WITHDRAWN

CONCORDIA UNIVERSITY

NK5308.A71939   C001 V
STAINED GLASS OF THE MIDDLE AGES IN

3 4211 000068708

S0-BSD-958

STAINED GLASS
OF THE MIDDLE AGES
IN ENGLAND & FRANCE

PLATE I.   THE ASCENSION WINDOW, LE MANS
Possibly Eleventh Century

STAINED GLASS
OF THE MIDDLE AGES
IN ENGLAND & FRANCE

BY

HUGH ARNOLD

WITH FIFTY PLATES IN COLOUR
BY
LAWRENCE B. SAINT

NEW YORK
THE MACMILLAN COMPANY

FIRST EDITION 1913   REPRINTED (DEMY 8VO) 1925
THIS EDITION 1939
REPRINTED 1955

MADE IN GREAT BRITAIN
PRINTED BY R. & R. CLARK, LIMITED, EDINBURGH

45439

PREFACE

THE Cathedral verger, conducting his flock of tourists round the building, while giving them plenty of really interesting and valuable information about it (for the verger of to-day is a different man from his predecessor, and is often very intelligent and well informed), remarks briefly, " The glass is of the thirteenth century "—or fourteenth or fifteenth, as the case may be; the procession gazes carelessly at it, and passes on. Yet from out of that dazzling and glowing labyrinth of coloured jewels a past age is speaking far more articulately, if one stops to unravel the message, than ever in stone or wood, and it is for those who can be induced to take that second look which will be followed by a third and a fourth and many more that I have written this book.

It is impossible in a book of this size to give an adequate review of all the important windows even

v

within the limits of place and time which I have set myself. I have therefore chosen for study certain typical windows in each century, and have written about them some of the things which interest me and which, I hope, will interest others.

The work of the countries and period I have chosen is of course the most important of all. There is beauty, it is true, in much Renaissance work (only a prig could resist the gaiety and charm of the windows of St. Vincent at Rouen), but it is for the most part beauty achieved in spite of, and not through, the material. There is beautiful mediæval work in Germany and Italy, but the Germans, till the Renaissance, clung to a rather lifeless and archaic convention, and the Italians were hampered by their greater knowledge of painting. The art has found its noblest expression in the work of the great school which for nearly the whole of the Middle Ages was common to France and England.

There is especial reason why we English should study the work of our own mediæval glass painters. They are the chief representatives of our primitive school of painting. It is true that there are English manuscripts in the museums, and there are the painted rood screens of Norfolk, including the superb example at Ranworth, and there is the portrait of Richard II. at Westminster ; but of the painting which must once have covered the walls of our churches, there is little left but patches of faded colour clinging here and there to the plaster, and the occasional dim outline of a figure.   Of our glass, on the other hand, in spite of four hundred years of destruction, a considerable quantity remains, and is worth far closer study than it has ever had.

I must gratefully acknowledge the help I have had from my brother, Mr. T. K. Arnold, especially in writing of the Canterbury glass of which he has made a very close study.   My thanks are also due to Mr. Noel Heaton for information on the chemical composition of glass.

The publishers are fortunate in having been able to reproduce, for the illustrations, the very beautiful coloured drawings of Mr. Lawrence B. Saint, which are now in the Victoria and Albert Museum.

H. A.

CONTENTS

LIST OF PLATES

xi

I

THE MAKING OF A WINDOW

1

THE MAKING OF A WINDOW

THE making of stained-glass windows is one of the arts which belong wholly to the Christian Era. Its traditions do not extend back beyond the great times of Gothic architecture, and it is to the work of those times that the student must turn, as the student of sculpture and architecture turns to that of the ancient world, to learn the basic principles of the art.

In the Middle Ages stained glass formed an important part, but still only a part, of that interior colour decoration without which no church was considered complete; but in spite of its fragile nature it has on the whole survived the attacks of time, the fury of the Puritan, the apathy and neglect of the eighteenth century, and the sinister energies of the nineteenth-century restorer better than the painting which once adorned the walls

3

and woodwork, and for this reason has come to be considered in these days as peculiarly appropriate to churches. So much so, indeed, that whereas I have sometimes found in country parishes a certain amount of opposition to any attempt to revive wall-painting as savouring of popery, no such feeling seems to exist with regard to coloured windows.

The process. Stained glass is not one of the arts in which the method of production reveals itself at the first glance. Indeed, so few people when looking at a stained-glass window, whether a gorgeous and solemn one of the thirteenth or fifteenth century, or a crude and vulgar one of the nineteenth, realize the long and laborious process by which the result, good or bad, has been obtained, that a short description of that process as finally perfected some five hundred years ago may not be out of place here.

One hears it so often spoken of as "painted glass"—Mr. Westlake calls his book *A History of Design in Painted Glass*—that it is not surprising that there should be a good deal of misconception on the point. It must be clearly understood then that the colour effects which are the glory of the art are not directly produced by painting at all, but by the window being built up of a multitude of small pieces of white and coloured glass—glass, that is, coloured in the making, and of which the artist must choose the exact shades he needs, cut them out to shape, and fit them together to form his design, using a separate piece for every colour or shade of colour.

In twelfth and thirteenth century windows many of these pieces are only half an inch wide and from one to two inches long, and few are bigger than the palm of one's hand; so the reader can amuse himself, if he wishes, in trying to calculate the number of pieces in one of the huge windows of this date in the Cathedral of Canterbury, York, or Chartres, and the labour involved in this, the initial stage of the process.

When the window is finished these pieces are put together like a puzzle and joined by grooved strips of lead soldered at the joints, just as any "lattice" window is put together (and until glass was made in large pieces this was the only way of filling a window); but before this is done the details of the design—features, folds of drapery, patterns, and so on—are painted on the glass in an opaque brownish enamel made of oxide of iron and other metals ground up with a "soft" glass (*i.e.*

glass with a low melting-point). This is mixed with oil or gum and water in order to apply it, and then the glass is placed in a kiln and "fired" till the enamel is fused on and, if well fired, becomes part of the glass itself. This is the only "painting" involved in the production of a stained-glass window, and its effect, in the hand of an artist, besides enabling him to express more than could be done merely with glass and lead, is to decorate and enrich what would otherwise be somewhat crude and papery in effect.

The two parts of the process. The process thus consists of two parts. The cutting and putting together of the glass is called *glazing*, and it is this that gives the window colour; while the enamel work is spoken of as *painting*, and gives detail, richness, and texture.

I shall presently show that the glazing and painting are really two separate crafts, having separate origins and development, and that stained glass as we know it, or as it should be called in strict accuracy "stained-and-painted" glass, is the product of their union.

There is another method, far inferior in the beauty of its results, by which pictures can be produced in glass, which is to paint on white glass with transparent coloured enamels. As, however, this method was not used till the seventeenth century, and is now once more almost wholly abandoned, it does not concern us here.

The softness of lead which makes it the only practicable metal for joining pieces of glass of complicated shapes, has the disadvantage that a stained-glass window when leaded up has a considerable degree of flexibility, and, if held by the edges alone, would be quite unable to resist the pressure of the wind, which on a big window is enormous,—think of the power even of a fresh breeze on a boat's sail.

It would not even be able to support its own weight for long, and so it follows that it must be held up by a system of short metal bars fixed firmly into the stone-work. Naturally the design of the window must be so arranged that these bars either do not interfere with it or form an integral part of it. In early windows, especially those of the twelfth and thirteenth centuries and even to some extent in those of the fourteenth, the bars are sufficiently important to form the governing factor in the design. *The iron-work.*

It must not be thought that stained glass loses in beauty by the presence of these black lines of lead and iron. On the contrary it gains enormously.

Large pieces of unrelieved colour in windows are thin in effect and trying to the eye, which needs the continual contrast of the solid black of the lead all over the window to enable it to appreciate the colour and brilliance of the glass. The painting when rightly used is directed to the same end, for it may be said that the smaller and more divided the spaces of clear glass, the more brilliant and jewel-like is the effect.

Silver stain.   To the rule that a separate piece of glass must be used for every change of colour, there are, in later work, two exceptions. The most important, which was discovered early in the fourteenth century, is the use of silver stain. It was then found that if white glass is painted with a preparation of silver—either oxide or chloride of silver will do—and then "fired" in the kiln used for the enamel painting, it will be stained a clear and indelible yellow, varying from pale lemon to deep orange, according to the strength of the painting.

Abrasion.   The other exception was Abrasion, effected by the use of what is called "flashed" glass. Flashed glass is glass so made that instead of being coloured all through, it consists of a thin film or "flash" of colour on a backing of white. With this glass it is possible to chip with a burin, or grind away, the

coloured film in places (we do it now with hydro-
fluoric acid) so as to get white and colour on the
same piece of glass.

In the Middle Ages only red and certain shades
of blue were made in this way, so the use of the
process was very much restricted.   The invention
of silver stain, on the other hand, by enabling the
artist to decorate his white glass and make it
interesting, led him at once to use a larger quantity
of white in his window, and so, as will be seen
later, had a considerable influence on design.

These, however, are the exceptions which prove
the rule, and, broadly speaking, a stained - glass
window must consist, to the eye, of flat patches of
colour, large or small, worked on with dark mono-
chromatic line work and shading.   These patches of
colour must each be separated from the next by a
black line—the leading—varying from a quarter to
half an inch in thickness, and crossed at intervals
by still thicker black lines—the iron bars.

It follows from this that anything like illusion Limitations
is impossible in stained glass, and no artist with any of the art.
sympathy for the medium would attempt it.   Un-
wise persons in decadent times have wasted much
ingenuity in the endeavour, but the result has
always been disastrous and ridiculous.   Apart from

its higher mission,—the expression of ideas and emotions,—which it shares with every other branch of art, the mission of stained glass is to beautify buildings and nothing else. It is the handmaid of architecture, and can only justify itself by loyal service of its mistress. The ideal of the stained-glass artist must not be a picture made transparent, but a window made beautiful.

Let no one suppose, however, that the artist is hampered by these limitations on the higher side of his work. On the contrary, they set him free to tell his story his own way. Ruskin—poor Ruskin, out of date, ridiculed, forgotten—pointed out long ago, in writing of Giotto's frescoes, the advantage which the pure colourist has over the chiaroscurist in his power of telling a story. In our times the fact has been rediscovered with a flourish of trumpets by the Post-Impressionists. I have no great enthusiasm, I confess, for the way in which they have carried out their principles, but I do know two perfect tellings of the story of the Creation. One is in mosaic on the ceiling of the narthex of St. Mark's at Venice, and the other is in the upper part of the east window of York Minster; and in each case the language used consists of flat forms and colour only.

II

THE BEGINNINGS OF STAINED GLASS

II

THE BEGINNINGS OF STAINED GLASS

I HAVE said that stained-glass work is the product of the union of two crafts, the glazier's and the enameller's. The glazier's work being the ground-work of a window, I will take it first.

What, to begin with, is glass? It is sand melted and run together. The best sand for the purpose is that which is most largely composed of the substance called silica, such as sand formed of powdered quartz, or flint. For some reason, the silica when melted does not recrystallize on cooling as might have been expected, but forms an even transparent substance, plastic while still hot. Think of the tremendous effect this one natural fact has had on the architecture, dress, and, probably, the physique of the nations of northern Europe.

Given sufficient heat, glass can be made by this

Glass-making.

13

means alone, but the heat required is so great that it has only been done in recent years for special purposes by means of the electric furnace. Failing this, the sand must be induced to melt at a lower temperature by means of a flux, for which either potash or soda may be used, and to which lime or lead must be added, to enable the glass to resist moisture. (Theophilus, describing the process in his Treatise, certainly no later than the thirteenth century, recommends the use of beech twigs calcined in an earthen pot, whence the name " Pot-ash.")

Colouring.   Glass may be coloured or " stained " while in a molten condition by the admixture of various substances, mostly metals, gold, copper, manganese, and so on, the result depending on the temperature to which it is subjected and on the exact composition of the glass as well as on the colouring matter used.

Blowing.   Glass is made into vessels, as most people know, by " blowing." The workman takes a dab of molten glass on the end of a long metal pipe, and putting his mouth to the pipe blows the glass —soap-bubble fashion—into a hollow bulb. Then by a rapid and dexterous series of alternate and repeated heating, blowing, and spinning, and manipulation with tools, most fascinating to watch, he shapes it into the form required.   If a flat sheet be required for window glass it may be run out flat when liquid, or blown as described above, and worked into a cylindrical form, split open, and un-rolled.   This is called "muff glass."   But glass can also be formed, by rapidly spinning it while soft, into a large flat disc, called a "crown," and is then known as "crown glass."   It was by these last two methods, the "muff" and the "crown," that all the material of the windows we have to consider in this book was made.

When cold, the sheet or disc of glass may be Cutting. cut to the shape required, either, as in the old days, by running a hot iron slowly along the proposed line of fracture, in which case a crack will follow the iron, or by scratching it with a diamond and then bending it so as to break along the line of the scratch.   The latter is a comparatively modern invention, and has in its turn been superseded by the use of a little steel wheel with a sharp edge.

Pliny gives a story of the invention of glass Pliny's story. which, if false, is still so picturesque that I cannot resist quoting it here.

A certain merchant-ship touched on the coast of Syria, and the crew landed near the mouth of the river Belus, on a beach of fine white sand which, Pliny says, was still in his day of great repute for glass-making. The ship's cargo consisted of natron,—a natural alkaline crystal which was much used in ancient times for washing,[1]—and the crew having lighted a fire on the sand used lumps of it from the cargo to prop up their kettle. What was their surprise to find afterwards a stream of molten glass running down from their camp-fire. In this case the natron acted as a flux and enabled the sand to melt in the heat of the camp-fire, which, however, must have been a very large and hot one.

Egyptian glass.

Now, whether this story is true or not, it cannot have been the beginning of more than a local industry, for the art of glass-making was known in Egypt from very early times indeed.

Its earliest use seems to have been in the imitation of precious stones, and perhaps for this reason it seems from the first to have been made in colours as well as in white; but the art of blowing it into vessels was certainly known in the fourth

[1] Pliny's word "nitrum" does not mean what we call nitre, which is potassium nitrate, but natron, or natural carbonate of soda, of which deposits are found in the Nile Delta. It is this that is meant in the passage in Jeremiah: "Though thou wash thee with nitre, and take thee much sope. . . ."

dynasty, and in some of the paintings in the tombs the process is actually represented.

It was not, however, till the first century of the Christian Era that any one seems to have thought of using glass to fill windows. In Egypt naturally the climate made it unnecessary, and even in Italy, where it can be cold enough in winter, civilization had evolved a style of architecture independent of glass.

Nevertheless it was introduced in Rome under the first emperors. Caligula had his palace windows glazed, and Seneca mentions it as one of the luxuries which had been introduced into life in his time, but which did not really add to a philosopher's happiness. Its introduction was, however, very gradual, and even two centuries later its use was still quoted as evidence of excessive luxuriousness.

Roman windows.

Remains of these Roman windows have been found at Pompeii and elsewhere. At Pompeii they are in the form of small panes of glass held, in one case in a wooden, and in another in a bronze lattice.[1] It must be remembered that large panes

---

[1] These panes are, I believe, of cast glass; but I have seen Roman window glass found at Silchester that was obviously " blown " glass and of very good quality.

2

were not available. Another method seems to have been to set panes of glass directly into small openings in stone-work.

When coloured glass was first used in windows we have no evidence to enable us to say. As, however, the manufacture of coloured glass was already a flourishing art it cannot have been long before the idea came of using it to decorate windows.

St. Sophia. Whether the windows of St. Sophia at Constantinople originally had colour in them or not, is not quite certain. That they were glazed we know, from the description of the church by Paul the Silentiary, an officer of Justinian's court, but his language about them is tantalizingly vague. From his enthusiasm at the effect of the sunlight through them I am inclined to suspect that they were coloured, though he does not definitely say so. Of this glass, which seems to have been fixed in small rectangular openings in a slab of alabaster, nothing, I believe, remains; but similar work—coloured—is to be seen in other mosques, the only difference being that the openings in the slab are formed into patterns and kept very small. (I have already mentioned the necessity, when dealing with *clear* coloured glass, of keeping the pieces small and contrasting them with plenty of solid dark.)

This was as far as stained glass in the East ever got. The Mahommedan conquerors seem to have taken the art as they found it, and continued it down without much change almost to modern times. Their religion debarred them from any attempt to represent living forms, so that the art as it stood sufficed for the needs of their architecture. Visitors to Leighton House may see some of these pierced and glazed lattices from Damascus, and very beautiful they are. In them the pieces are not much larger than a penny, and are set in holes cut in plaster slabs, bevelled on the inside, the glass being set at the outer edge of the hole. The glass is not really of very good quality, but treated in this way even thin poor glass looks rich and jewel-like.

What course the glazier's art first followed in the West it is impossible to say, for nothing of it remains earlier than the eleventh century, if as early. Nevertheless, in spite of repeated barbarian invasions, it seems never to have quite died out.

The Church, the refuge of the arts and civilization in the general debacle, sheltered it, and from being the luxury of the Roman millionaire it became the ornament of the house of God. From time to time we get allusions to glazed windows,

Mahommedan windows.

Glass in the West.

but never a description that can throw much light on their construction or design. Enough is said, however, to show that coloured glass was sometimes used. For instance, we read that St. Gregory of Tours placed coloured windows in the Church of St. Martin in that city in the sixth century.

One or two facts, however, lead me to think that whereas, in the East, glass was set in stone or plaster, in the West it was usually set in metal. At Pompeii, as we have seen, panes of glass are set in a bronze lattice and fixed with nuts and screws. As colour was introduced it is probable that from the necessity, already spoken of, of keeping the pieces small, several bits would be joined together with lead to fill one opening of the rigid lattice, and so patterns could be formed. Leo of Ostia says his predecessor, the Abbot Desiderius, filled the windows of the Chapter-House at Monte Cassino in the eleventh century with coloured glass, " glazed with lead and fixed with iron "; and certain it is that the earliest existing windows consist of a large rigid lattice of massive rebated iron bars, in which leaded panels have been placed separately, and held there by light cross-bars passed through staples and keyed with wedges.

If this conjecture is correct, we may assume

that the art of the glazier had for some time been perfected, and had progressed as far as was possible for it unaided, when its union, probably in the tenth century, with that of the enameller gave birth to the art of "stained-and-painted" glass— that is, stained glass as we know it.

Without the use of enamel the glazier's craft *The opaque* must always have been strictly limited to patterns *enamel.* in glass and lead, or, as we now call it, "plain glazing." What was needed to convert it into the art as we know it was the addition of painting in the black or brown monochrome enamel described in the first chapter.

Only one who has worked in glass, and seen his work grow from a map-like combination of white and coloured glass to the finished glass painting, knows the power the enamel gives him of controlling, softening, and enriching his effects of colour. The power it gives of suggesting form is only one, and not the most important, of its functions, and it was as vital to the work of the twelfth and thirteenth as of the fifteenth century. With its introduction the glorious windows of the Middle Ages became possible.

Exactly when and where the application of the enameller's craft to glass windows first took place it is impossible to say with certainty; but there is some reason to suppose that it was in France, and not earlier than the tenth century.

Venetian
enamellers.
Enamel—the art of painting on metal with an easily fusible glass ground to powder, which is then fused on to its groundwork in a furnace—was of ancient invention, and had been carried to a high state of perfection in Constantinople in the eighth and following centuries. Thence by way of Venice it had come to France, where a colony of Venetian craftsmen had established itself before the end of the tenth century.

Monkswear-
mouth.
France was already famous for its glaziers: for instance, when in A.D. 680 the Abbot, Benedict Biscop, glazed the windows of the monastery at Monkswearmouth, we read in Bede that "he sent messengers to Gaul to fetch makers of glass (or rather artificers) till then unknown in Britain. . . . They came, and not only finished the work required, but taught the English nation their handicraft"; and it is probable that the French glaziers, chafing under the limitations of their art, called in the aid of the Venetian enamellers. It is noteworthy that no attempt seems to have been made to use transparent coloured enamel on glass. That mistake was reserved for the decadence of the art seven

hundred years later.   Perhaps experiment con-
vinced them that enamel colour could never hope
to rival the depth and richness of coloured glass, and
the glazier would realize that what he wanted of
the enameller was not colour but black, to modify
and enrich the colour which his glass already gave
him in full measure.   In this book, therefore, the
word "enamel," when used in connection with
glass, must be understood to refer, unless coloured
enamel is specifically mentioned, to this brown
opaque enamel or "paint," as glass-workers call it.

But the enameller's art had another influence on Cloisonné
that of stained glass.   A form of enamelling developed at Constantinople and practised at Limoges
was that known as "cloisonné."   In this, narrow
strips of metal are soldered edgeways to the ground-
work and the spaces between are filled with differently coloured enamel, the different colours being
thus separated by strips of metal.

When the enameller's attention was first turned
to glasswork, in which different coloured pieces of
glass were separated by strips of lead, he must have
been struck with the similarity of the two arts, and
have perceived that the style of design already
developed in enamel could be applied with little
change to glasswork.

This probably explains not only the apparently sudden birth of the art fully formed, but the strongly Byzantine character of the design in the earliest work, the enameller's art having been brought, as we have seen, from Constantinople by way of Venice.[1]

What, then, is the oldest "stained-and-painted" glass in existence? At Brabourne in Kent there is a small window, of which a coloured tracing may be seen in South Kensington Museum, which may belong to the eleventh century. It consists of a simple pattern of white glass and leading, with small pieces of colour inserted at intervals. Some of these latter, however, have been formed into rosettes of simple design by means of opaque enamel, which is the only painting in the window at all. Whatever the actual date of the window, I think it is not unlikely that it shows the manner in which enamel painting and glazing were first combined.

Early window at Le Mans.

Almost the earliest glass, however, to which any date can be approximately assigned are the panels

---

[1] By some writers it has been claimed that the whole idea of stained-glass work was derived from cloisonné enamel; but from the fact that the glazing of windows in glass and metal had been known long before, I think the course of events I have suggested above to have been more probable.

in Le Mans Cathedral,[1] which are illustrated by a sketch of Mr. Saint's in Plate I.

In a thirteenth century manuscript preserved at Le Mans it is recorded that Bishop Hoel, who occupied the See from A.D. 1081 to 1097, glazed the windows of the Cathedral with stained glass, " sumptuosa artis varietate," and it is just possible that this glass, which was found in 1850 scattered and glazed up among fragments of a later date, may be part of the glass referred to.

It seems to have formed the lower part of a window representing the Ascension, and consists of figures of the Virgin and the Twelve Apostles " gazing up into Heaven."

The arrangement is very simple. There seems to have been little or no ornament in the window, and the figures in white and coloured draperies, standing on conventionalized hillocks which represent the top of the " high mountain," are relieved against a background of plain colour in alternate panels of red and blue. In this window and for long afterwards the background represents nothing in nature, but merely serves the purpose of throwing up and isolating the figures.

[1] There is some at Augsburg and at Tegernsee in Bavaria which may perhaps be a little earlier, but it is not certain.

As the glass is not in its original position, one can only guess at its original construction and design.   All early windows, as I have said, consisted of separate leaded panels inserted into the openings of a massive metal framework, an arrangement which of necessity governed the design.   In this case one would expect the six panels, with their differently coloured backgrounds, each to have filled a separate opening in the framework.

If this is so, however, the panels must have been somewhat cut down, since as at present glazed the limbs and drapery of the figures occasionally overlap into the neighbouring panels. I think it very probable indeed that the glass has been so cut down, and that the window at Poitiers, illustrated in Plate II., though of later date, gives a true idea of the original relation of these panels to the iron-work.   It is probable too that the upper part of the Le Mans window was filled with a figure of the ascending Christ on the same plan as that of Poitiers.   It is, indeed, only fair to say that the Poitiers window, which is of the end of the twelfth century, throws some doubt on the greater antiquity of that at Le Mans.

There is little or no ornament in the latter, and perhaps there was never much, though it may have

once had simple borders between the panels and
a rich border like that at Poitiers (not shown
in the drawing) surrounding the whole. The
technique followed in the painting is precisely
that which obtained for nearly three hundred
years after. That is to say, as far as possible the
effect is obtained by glazing, and the features and
folds of drapery are put in with strong, dark,
sweeping lines of enamel. The style of the
drawing, however, both in the figures and the
drapery, is perhaps more purely Byzantine than
any later work. The sweeping lines of the
drapery are graceful and decorative, but the
action of the figures is absolutely conventional.
There is none of that feeling for motion which,
expressed in line, gives so much vigour and
animation to the subject windows of the thirteenth
century.

In colour, however, which after all is the most
important thing in a window, this glass is splendid,
and for the quality of the material and the way
in which it has resisted the attacks of time it is
superior to much glass of a later date.

45439

III

THE STYLE OF THE FIRST PERIOD

III

THE STYLE OF THE FIRST PERIOD

STAINED glass from its birth to the Renaissance has been divided by Winston into three main periods, each having broad characteristics peculiar to itself, and which he named after the corresponding architectural styles, Early English, Decorated, and Perpendicular. As, however, these terms only apply to English work, and as the architectural styles do not altogether correspond in date with those of the glass, I prefer to speak simply of the First, Second, and Third Period.

The First lasts from the earliest examples almost to the end of the thirteenth century, and might be subdivided again into twelfth and thirteenth century work, between which there is a distinct difference.

The three periods.

The Second covers nearly the whole of the fourteenth century.

The Third lasts down to the end of the fifteenth century, by which time the influence of the classic Renaissance began to be felt in glasswork, but lingers on in belated examples well into the sixteenth.

Between each of these periods there is a very short transitional period lasting hardly a decade, and occupying the closing years of each century.

It must not be thought, however, that at any time design in stained glass stood still. Its history is rather one of periodic impulses, due no doubt to the work of individual genius, followed in each case by a long and gradual decline, towards the end of which artists began to grow restless and feel about for new modes of expression, and so prepare the way for the next impulse of genius.

The First Period.

The broad characteristics then which distinguish the First Period are—

(1) Its rich colour.

(2) Its mosaic character.

(3) The importance of the iron-work and its influence on the design.

(4) The method of painting.

Its rich colour.

(1) *Its Colour.*—The colour of the glass in this First Period is of a barbaric richness, unequalled in the succeeding periods. A very deep and splendid

blue is used, in contrast with the greyish-blue of later glass, and it is of an uneven tint, which greatly adds to its quality. The ruby,[1] too, is often of a streaky character and of great beauty. These two usually form the dominant colours in the window, the greens, yellows, and purples being used rather to relieve them.

So much is the artist in love with his deep reds and blues, which he nearly always uses for the backgrounds of his figures, that he seldom insults them by painting on them except in so far as is necessary to the drawing, reserving his enamel mainly for the decoration of his whites and paler colours, keeping them in their places by a delicate fret of line and pattern work.

It is only towards the latter part of the period, when the quality of the glass began to fail a little, that he ever covered the whole surface of a blue background with an enamelled diaper, to give it a depth and richness which was lacking in the glass itself.

Except in the grisaille windows to be described later, in which a definitely white effect is aimed at,

---

[1] It seems to have been the practice of glass-workers in the Middle Ages to describe the different colours in glass by the jewel they most nearly resembled. A survival of this at the present day is their universal habit of calling red glass " ruby."

the amount of colour used in proportion to the white glass is considerably greater than in succeeding periods. Nevertheless the white is always present, running everywhere among the colour like a silver thread, relieving and beautifying it. In fact it was not till modern times that any glass-worker ever thought he could do without it.

Its mosaic character.

(2) *The Mosaic Character of the Glass.*—The designer depends for his effect primarily upon glass and lead, and builds up his window out of tiny pieces. He had learned the jewel-like effect this gave to his work, and seemed to grudge no labour in it. Take, for example, the Ark at Canterbury in Plate IV. Where a fifteenth century painter would have been content to make the ark of perhaps only one piece of glass, probably of white, getting his detail in enamel and silver stain only, our thirteenth century craftsman has used over fifty pieces, purple, blue, red, yellow, green and white, and that in a space less than a foot square! He was a colourist par excellence, and his waves, too, are blue, greenish-blue and green, with caps of white foam—all a mosaic of glass and lead.

From this dependence for its effect on the actual material used, it follows that the work of no period is more easily damaged than this by so-called "restoration." The introduction of only half a dozen pieces of crudely coloured modern glass is often enough to upset the whole harmony of the colour and to make the window irritating instead of restful to the eye. In France, indeed, so few windows of this period have been left unrestored that the period does not always get justice done it. I doubt if many people honestly get much pleasure from the effect of the windows of the Sainte Chapelle at Paris taken as a whole; but if you notice how much of the original glass is in South Kensington Museum you will understand the reason.

(3) *The Influence of Iron-Work.*—The windows The iron-work. of this period consisted from the first, as we have seen, of separate leaded panels inserted into the openings of an iron lattice. This lattice was formed of iron bars of a T-shaped section, the head of the T being outwards, and having staples at intervals on the inner rib, through which light iron bars were thrust and keyed with wedges, to hold the glass in its place.

In the absence of any tracery to assist in the support of the glass, this iron-work in large windows was of a massive character and could not be disregarded in the design. In figure work there were two possible ways of dealing with it: one was to make the figures so large as to be independent of it; and the other was to make the figures so small that a complete figure-subject could be included in one opening of the frame work.

Both these methods were used by the artists of the early period. Where the work is far from the eye, as in the clerestory windows, we usually find large single figures—far larger, often, than life— filling the whole window, like the big angel from Chartres on Plate X. and the smaller and older figure of Methuselah from Canterbury on Plate III. When, on the other hand, the work is near the eye, as in the aisle windows, they used the other method, filling each opening of the iron-work with a small subject-panel like that of Noah and the Dove in Plate IV., thus producing what is called the medallion window.

Medallion windows.

At first the lattice work consisted merely of upright and horizontal bars. These, it is true, sometimes, as in the twelfth century window at Poitiers in Plate II., were manipulated to fit the subject, but more usually the subject fitted the bars.

Bent iron-work.

In the earliest form of medallion window, such as those in the west windows at Chartres and some

of the earliest ones at Canterbury, the window is
divided by the iron-work into a series of regular
squares, each of which alternately is filled with a
square and a circular figure-subject.   Later, however, in the thirteenth century, the iron-work
itself was bent into geometric patterns which
the medallions were shaped to fit, producing the
elaborate designs shown in the insets of the
whole windows in Plates IV. and VIII. from
Canterbury.

Even when in the latter part of the thirteenth
century there was a return, prompted no doubt
by motives of economy, to iron-work composed
of straight bars, the influence of these elaborate
lattices is still seen in the shapes of the medallions,
though these are no longer outlined by the iron-
work which now passes across or between them.
An example of this is shown in Plate XIV. from
Rouen Cathedral.

(4) *The Method of Painting.*—This consists of The method
vigorous line work in the brown enamel, laid on of painting.
with a brush in beautiful, firm, expressive strokes
on a ground of clear glass.   Lettering and patterns
are formed by being scratched out clear from a
solid coat of enamel.   There is no attempt at
modelling in planes or at light and shade, and

half-tone is only used, as I shall presently explain, to soften the edges of the line work.

Irradiation.   Now the optical law which most affects the technique of stained glass is that of which the effect is known as "irradiation." In an unscientific work it is enough to say that it is the law which causes the filament of an electric light, in reality thin as a hair, to appear when incandescent as thick as a piece of worsted. In the same way it makes the clear spaces of glass appear larger than they really are in proportion to the obscured parts, and also tends to make them look rounded.

From the fact that the glass between the line work was left nearly clear, the work of this period is more affected by irradiation than any other, and the artist had to make his line work very black and thick in order to tell at all, especially in work far from the eye. For instance, if he wished to distinguish the fingers of a hand he separated them with solid black spaces as thick as the fingers themselves.

The line   The glass between the line work is left nearly work.   clear, but not quite ; for if quite clear the intensity of the light would have bitten into the edge of the black line and made it appear what engravers call a "rotten" line, or even be invisible altogether at a little distance. Therefore the painter softened the edges of his line work by one of two methods. The first, described by Theophilus, though I cannot say for certain that it has been used in any glass I have examined, was to slightly smear the painting when wet with a soft brush. The other, which seems to have been more used, was to edge the dark line work, so to speak, with fainter strokes in semi-transparent half-tone. In work that was meant to be placed near the eye the line work is extraordinarily fine and delicate, while in work that has to be seen from a distance, such as the clerestory windows of a cathedral, we find the whole scale of the execution increased. Lines are there used from half an inch to an inch thick, but in every case the work is equally admirable for its precision and vigour.

In the later periods the half-tone shading The "Matt." became developed into the "matt" or thin coat of enamel laid evenly all over the surface of the glass, from which, when dry, the lights were brushed out and the line work became more and more delicate. Still, as long as technique remained sound, the strength of shading was really obtained by line work, the matt or half-tone serving its true use in softening the light and making the line work visible.

Renaissance glass painters, in their efforts to produce the effects of oil painting in glass, tried to get rid of the effect of irradiation altogether by dulling the whole surface of the glass, with fatal results to the beauty of the material.

To sum up, although the work of this period may suffer in popular esteem from the drawing being conceived in an archaic convention,—a convention different to our own,—and from having suffered from restoration, the fact remains that at no time did the artist understand better the possibilities and limitations of his art and adopt a sounder technique in regard to them.

IV

TWELFTH CENTURY GLASS

IV

TWELFTH CENTURY GLASS

THE few examples I have mentioned are the only ones which can with any probability be dated from the eleventh century, but of twelfth century work much more remains.

The window at Poitiers in Plate II. shows little Poitiers. if any change in style from the Le Mans window in Plate I. It is still almost pure Byzantine, and if I were to judge by style alone I should place this window very early indeed. A fragment of an inscription has, however, been found on it— DITHANC . . . BLAS,—which has been thought to mean that the window was the gift of one Maurice de Blason, who became Bishop of Poitiers in 1198. If so, and if we are right in identifying the Le Mans window with Bishop Hoel's glazing, a whole century separates the two.

The probable explanation is that the Byzantine

43

style had lingered on in the south-east of France, as it may well have done, whereas north of the Loire a school had by this time arisen, and had been flourishing for many years, which was producing work both in France and England of a very different and far more advanced character.

The school of Chartres, St. Denis, and Canterbury. The twelfth and early thirteenth century windows at Chartres, St. Denis, Canterbury and Sens show such resemblance to each other that there can be little doubt of their common origin. As, however, their execution covers a period of at least seventy years, one man cannot have been responsible for them all.

Probably they represent the work of a group of men working together—perhaps never more than half a dozen at one time—under a master who was trained by his predecessor, and who in turn would be succeeded in the leadership by the best of his pupils. Several of these masters in succession must have been men of genius, and thus between them they evolved a style which, carried on by a succession of lesser men, governed design in stained glass for a century to come.

The rise of this school is the first of the periodic impulses to which I have referred, and the work they produced was, for its dignity and grandeur, unequalled for two hundred years—if it has ever been equalled at all.

The figure of Methuselah **or** " Matusale " in Plate III., which is one of the few remaining of the original figures once in the choir clerestory at Canterbury (it is now in the S. Transept), is a good example of their work, and a comparison of it with the Poitiers window (which is actually later in date but in the older style) shows the greatness of the change they effected. The change is, in fact, that from ancient to modern art: from Byzantine, the last lingering survival of the great classic tradition of Greece, to Gothic, the first expression of the art of the modern world.

Who were these men and where did they come from ? Some would have it that there was a great central school at Chartres, but there is little evidence for it. When Abbot Suger built the great abbey of St. Denis, which was dedicated in 1142, he filled it with glass, " painted," says his secretary, Monk William, " with exquisite art by many masters of *divers nations* " (" de diversis nationibus "). Does this mean that some of them were English or Germans, or only men from other provinces than the Ile de France ? No one can say ; but they must have been working together to produce the results they did.   One statement of the Monk William's leads me to think that the work was done on the spot.   He says the work was very costly, because they " used sapphires to colour their glass."   Now this is an obvious misunderstanding, due to the practice, in those days, of describing coloured glass by the name of the precious stone it resembled, and such a mistake is most likely to have been made in conversation with the artists themselves.

It is, of course, always possible that they had no permanent headquarters but took up their abode in whatever city their chief work was for the time being, there erected their furnaces, which the description of Theophilus shows to have been simple affairs, and remained there till their work was completed—which must have taken some years in every case—and then moved on to the next work.

Much has been made of the fact that a window in Rouen bears the signature of one Clement of Chartres,—" Clemens vitrearius Carnutensis me fecit,"—but that window is a hundred and forty years later than St. Denis.   By that time the whole Cathedral at Chartres had been filled with glass, a task which extended over thirty years; and Clement may well have learned his trade and passed from apprentice to master there. No other artist of the school has signed his name anywhere, nor has Clement anywhere else.

One can tell pretty well the order in which the most important of their work which remains was done. First Chartres and St. Denis,—so near together that one cannot say which came first,—then Canterbury, Sens, and then back to Chartres again, where a fire had destroyed all but the west windows. This, however, probably represents only a small portion of their labours, of which the rest has disappeared. For instance, a few fragments set among later work in York Minster have all the characteristics of this school; and we know that Prior Conrad's choir at Canterbury, which was completed in 1130 and destroyed in 1175, was renowned for the splendour of its glass, which may have been their work too.

A window at Le Mans, rather later than the one illustrated, and which Mr. Westlake thinks may be dated about 1120, shows signs of the new movement. It consists of a series of subjects from the stories of SS. Gervasius and Protasius, and already shows the arrangement of small medallions of simple shape, surrounded by ornament filling the rectangular openings of the iron-work, though from the fact that some of the medallions seem to have been cut down, they are probably not in their original position. In the drawing of the subjects the artist is breaking away from the Byzantine tradition. The new wine is bursting the old bottles. He is a man in love with life, and when he depicts a group of men stoning a saint he likes to make them really throwing, and to show in their faces, as well as he knows how, that they are thorough ruffians.

Next in antiquity to this window, and some twenty or thirty years later (1142–1150), come the earliest of the windows at Chartres and at St. Denis.

Chartres.   In the year A.D. 1134 a terrible fire destroyed the town of Chartres and so damaged the west end of the Cathedral that it had to be pulled down and rebuilt—a work which took some fifteen years to accomplish, while the towers were not finished till twenty years later still. The three windows over the west door were filled with glass some time between 1145 and 1150.

The west windows.   In early times churches seem to have been peculiarly liable to destruction by fire, owing perhaps to the number of wooden buildings by which they were surrounded. The early history of

LAWRENCE B. SAINT. 1911

PLATE II.

PART OF
CRUCIFIXION
WINDOW,
POITIERS

Late Twelfth
Century

PLATE III.
METHUSELAH,
CANTERBURY,
ORIGINALLY
IN CHOIR
CLERESTORY
Twelfth Century

every great cathedral is one of successive disastrous conflagrations, after each of which the building rises once more, larger and more splendid. Thus, in 1194, another fire completely destroyed the whole of the Cathedral with the exception of the newly built west end, which included the three windows in question. These escaped damage, protected perhaps by the immense depth of their embrasures, and still remain almost unimpaired to this day, the largest and most perfect windows of their time that have come down to us. In them one feels that the new movement has found itself and produced a great man.

Two of them, the central one, which is the largest, being some 30 feet high and 10 wide, and that on the south, are medallion windows, containing scenes from the life of Christ. The bars of the iron-work, which are about 3 feet apart, divide them into a series of regular squares, which are filled with square and circular medallions; in the central window the figures in the medallions are relieved against alternate backgrounds of ruby and blue. The ruby of the twelfth and thirteenth centuries is a wonderful colour. It is never of a perfectly even tint, each piece having, as it were, its own character, and the colour seems to have

4

a slightly granulated or "crumbly" texture, which gives it a quality unknown in later glass. So beautiful was it evidently considered that the artist seldom or never attempted to enrich it with painting.

The Jesse tree. The third window, that on the north, is filled with a "Tree of Jesse."

The subjects of stained-glass windows in this First Period were chosen with one object—the exposition of the Christian Doctrine, and of this the human descent of Christ was an essential part. Accordingly, at all periods in the history of mediæval stained glass we find windows devoted to the representation of "the Tree of Jesse."

The arrangement is always the same as in this window at Chartres. The figure of Jesse lies recumbent at the foot of the window, and from his loins rises the "Tree"—a mass of branching scroll work with conventional foliage, spreading over the whole window, carrying on its branches David and other human ancestors of Christ, and culminating in the Virgin and Christ Himself at the top of the window. On either side are ranged the Prophets who foretold His coming, and the whole, surrounded by a rich border, forms, at Chartres, a mass of jewelled colour some 9 feet wide and 25 feet high.

This window and the one of which a part, identical in design, remains at St. Denis, are the oldest examples I know of a Jesse tree in stained glass, and whether or not they were the first to be made, their design formed a model for others for long after.

The remainder of the windows in the Cathedral, including the western rose, are of the thirteenth century with one exception—the one in the south choir aisle, which contains the great figure of the Virgin known as "Notre Dame de la Belle Verrière": the only window, as far as I know, to which in former times people knelt by hundreds in adoration, and before which they still occasionally burn a candle.

The Virgin with the Child on her knee sits enthroned in the upper part of the window, and surrounded by angels, on a much smaller scale, incensing and holding candles, while below are medallions illustrating the Marriage at Cana and the Temptation. The angels and the medallions are of the thirteenth century, but the figures of the Virgin and Child with their background are almost certainly of the twelfth. Probably the veneration in which they were held caused them to be rescued from the fire,—hurriedly broken out, perhaps, from the surrounding glass,—and then reset in thirteenth century work after the Cathedral was rebuilt.[1] The Virgin is dressed in a robe of pale greyish-blue, of a colour one seldom sees in later work, relieved against a background of deep ruby, set with jewels of a darker blue. The precision of the colour harmony is wonderful, and no drawing I have seen of the window gives, even in outline, the beautiful poise of the head, bent in gracious benediction.

Although I have said that the workers of this school were breaking away from the Byzantine tradition and looking at life with their own eyes, yet it is never possible for men suddenly to produce work wholly independent of tradition, even when they are foolish enough to try ; so we find in this case Greek art, through Byzantine, retains enough influence with these men to give to their work a dignity and restraint which is lacking in that of the thirteenth century. This is very noticeable wherever one gets the two in close juxtaposition, as at Chartres and also at Canterbury. There is an impressive severity of design and a feeling for proportion in the figure of the Virgin in La Belle

[1] Some critics have thought the figure merely a copy from an earlier design, but I cannot agree with them.

Verrière which one misses in the surrounding work, which, though very beautiful, is by comparison small and fussy in treatment.

In the meantime, in 1142, while the west front St. Denis. of Chartres Cathedral was still in progress, the great Abbot Suger had finished the construction of his abbey of St. Denis, near Paris. He was a great patron of the arts, as well as a good man and the first statesman of his age, and he seems to have spared no pains in the decoration of the church and especially in the filling of the windows with stained glass. Of this glass, alas! only the merest remnant is left, consisting of several medallions and part of a "Tree of Jesse." They have been collected and placed in the chapels of the apse of the church, embedded in garishly coloured ornament — the work of M. Gérente, acting under the orders of the great and terrible Viollet-le-Duc—which effectually prevents one taking any pleasure in their beauty. They are, however, very interesting to study. Whether or not they were done before or after the three windows at Chartres it is, I think, impossible to say for certain. The history of the two buildings shows that they must have been done within a few years of each other (two of those at St. Denis

contain figures of Suger as donor, and he died in
1152), and they are certainly the work of the same
school. The Jesse tree in particular is either a
copy, or the original, on a smaller scale, of the one
at Chartres, being almost identical in design.

Many of the medallions are interesting from
their deeply symbolical character. In one, for
instance, is Christ, with the seven gifts of the
Holy Spirit, represented, as in the Jesse tree, by
doves, each contained in a circle and connected
with His breast by rays. With His left hand He
unveils a figure labelled " Synagoga," and with His
right He crowns another figure labelled " Ecclesia."

Another very curious medallion represents the
fœderis arca, "ark of the covenant." A figure of
the Almighty supports a crucifix which rises from
the ark,—a square box on four wheels,—while round
about are the four symbols of the Evangelists.
The cross is thus shown as the symbol of God's
new covenant with man as the ark was that of
the old. A quaint feature is that the artist, while
feeling that all four wheels had got to be shown
somehow, has been in some difficulty as to how to
show the farther pair, and has therefore placed
them above the ark, as if resting on it, as an
ancient Egyptian artist might have done in his place.

In most of the medallions the teaching of the subject is emphasized and the application pointed out by rhyming Latin hexameters, doggerel in style and innocent of prosody, such as:

Quod Moyses velat, Christi doctrina revelat.

The same feature is found in the glass at Canterbury. None of the verses are identical, but the literary style is the same.

At Angers there are some remains of twelfth century windows which are thought to be about the same date as those of Chartres and St. Denis, or even a little earlier, and there are some at Chalons, but they cannot be dated with any exactitude, and I have had no opportunity of examining them. Next after these in point of date should, I think, come the earliest of the windows at Canterbury, though nearly thirty years must separate the two.

Angers and Chalons.

A few fragments in York Minster, however, show where the artists may have been occupied meantime. There are some scraps in the clerestory —scraps of a Jesse window of which the details are almost identical with the St. Denis work—and a medallion representing Daniel in the Lion's Den, which is glazed into the foot of the centre light

Fragments at York.

of the great thirteenth century grisaille windows in the north transept, known as "the Five Sisters." It is a circular medallion filled out to a square form with ornament, no doubt to fit a square of the iron-work, and strongly resembles the St. Denis work.

Canterbury choir. Of the stained glass of the twelfth and thirteenth centuries, which was once the glory of Canterbury Cathedral, only a remnant has escaped the zeal of the Puritans. The minister placed in charge of the Cathedral under the Commonwealth, one Richard Culmer, known to his enemies as "Blue Dick," though I do not know why, relates with glee how he stood on a ladder sixty steps high with a whole pike in his hand and "rattled down proud Beckett's glassie bones."

I own I feel less resentment against "Blue Dick," who at least thought the windows important enough to smash, than against that later vandal Wyatt, who in the eighteenth century sold the glass at Salisbury for the price of the lead in it, or those who even now in many places are letting old glass perish for want of proper care.

Even "Blue Dick" seems to have tired of his pious labours before they were quite finished, for, of the early windows, he has left us two in the north

PLATE IV.
"NOË IN ARCHA,"
FROM THE NORTH
CHOIR AISLE,
CANTERBURY
Twelfth Century

choir aisle, and four in the Trinity Chapel east of the choir, in which most of the old glass remains. Besides these there are many medallions and numerous fragments scattered about in other windows and embedded in the work of the modern restorer, and several large figures from the clerestory, of which the Methuselah in Plate III., now in the south transept, is one.

In the year 1174, four years after Becket's death, the splendid choir built by Prior Conrad in 1130 was completely destroyed by fire, and the monks immediately set about building a new one. Gervase the monk has left a detailed account of the progress of the great work, year by year and pillar by pillar, for the space of ten years, first under the French master-builder, William of Sens, and then under his successor, William the Englishman ("little in body but in workmanship of many kinds acute and honest"), so that we know just when each part of the work was finished. Now in the spring of 1180, he relates, the monks had a great desire to celebrate Easter in the new choir, and to gratify them the master, by a special effort, succeeded in getting the building finished and roofed in almost to the east end of the choir, where he placed a hoarding to keep out the weather.

Since we are told that in this hoarding there were three glass windows, it seems reasonable to suppose that the other windows were glazed too. Now since both the windows in the north choir aisle and, when in its original position, the Methuselah on Plate III. were well to the westward of the point at which the hoarding was erected, I have no doubt that they were in position by this date, in which opinion I am confirmed by the character of the glass itself. That in the Trinity Chapel to the east of the hoarding would naturally be later.

The same arrangement seems to have been followed at Canterbury as elsewhere of having large figures in the clerestory and small medallions in the lower windows.

The Methuselah, which seems to have formed one of a series of Patriarchs,—of which three others remain, which filled the windows in the clerestory of the choir,—is a particularly dignified figure, and it is noticeable that the throne he is seated on is of somewhat the same type as that of Notre Dame de la Belle Verrière at Chartres. As in all windows of this date, the flesh is executed in glass of a brownish-pink colour instead of white, which later on became the rule.

This illustration shows very well the early method of painting. Where possible, as in the rich blue of the background, the glass is left quite clear. The folds of the drapery and the features are drawn in sure and vigorous line work. Diaper is used very sparingly, only when it is necessary to "keep back" and subdue a piece of glass, as in the case of the green cushion to the throne and the border of the tunic. If you can imagine the glass with these pieces left clear or with any other piece diapered, you will see how unerring has been the artist's judgment.[1]

The letters of the inscription are scratched out of a dark ground of enamel. This is the invariable method used in early glass, which indeed is always (except in grisaille, of which more later) conceived as a light design on a dark ground. In the fifteenth century the reverse was the case, and then we get inscriptions in dark lettering on a light ground.

The arched form of the top of the background shows how it once fitted a clerestory light, though doubtless with a border, and the space above has been filled with scroll work of, I think, the same date, which may have come from some of the medallion windows in the choir aisles.

[1] The little piece of white with yellow stain under the right toe is, of course, a fifteenth century scrap.

The two medallion windows in the north choir aisle formed part, as we know from an old MS. still in existence, of a series of twelve dealing with the life and parables of our Lord.

In style they very closely resemble the St. Denis work, perhaps a little further developed. Some of the medallions, indeed, are almost identical with those at St. Denis, notably that of the Magi on horseback following the star. The figures are tall and dignified, and both for drawing and decorative placing are far better than much work of the succeeding century. The Calling of Nathaniel is a particularly good panel.

The westernmost of the two windows still retains the early arrangement found at Chartres, the iron-work consisting simply of straight bars dividing it into a series of regular squares, which are filled alternately with circular and square medallions.

The other one of the two has bent iron-work of a very simple design, consisting simply of four circles connected by straight bars, thus marking the transition from one form to another; which is another reason for dating these windows between the west windows of Chartres, where the iron-work is all straight, and those at Sens, where it is nearly all

PLATE V. THE ENTOMBMENT, FROM THE EAST WINDOW, CANTERBURY
Twelfth or early Thirteenth Century

bent. The small scale-sketch in the corner of Plate IV. shows the arrangement of the iron-work and the medallions. The panel of Noah in the Ark is from one of the semicircles on the left side of the window. The spaces between the medallions are filled up with beautiful foliated scroll work, on a ruby ground of the same character as that round the head of Methuselah.

The arrangement of their subjects is so interesting, forming one of the first and most complete examples of a "type and antitype" window, that I shall describe it in some detail.

In each of these two windows the upper two-thirds, or thereabouts, of the glass is in its original position, while the lower panels, smashed by the pike of "Blue Dick," who seems at this point to have got tired of going up his ladder, have been filled with subjects from other windows of the series.

Down the centre run the subjects from the life of Christ, while on each side are the "types" or subjects from the Old Testament which illustrate it. Thus the westernmost of the two, once the second of the series, begins at the top with the Magi following the star, while on one side is Balaam, with the words of his prophecy, "There shall come a star out of Jacob, etc.," and on the

other Isaiah, with the words, " The Gentiles shall
come to Thy light, and kings to the brightness of
Thy rising."

Next below we see in the centre the arrival of
the Magi before Herod, illustrated on the left by
the Israelites coming out of Egypt, led by Moses,
and on the right by the Gentiles leaving a heathen
temple containing an idol—a naked blue figure
(blue merely because the artist wanted some blue
there), and following Christ, by way of a font,
towards a Christian altar, while a demon above
their heads urges them to return to the idol.   As
at St. Denis, each of the medallions has a Latin
rhyme attached, explaining and enforcing the
lesson.   Here, for instance, it runs :

> Stella Magos duxit et eos ab Herode reduxit,
> Sic Satanam gentes fugiunt te Christe sequentes.

Next we see the Magi making their offerings
to the infant Christ, on one side of which is the
Queen of Sheba visiting Solomon and on the other
Joseph in Egypt receiving his suppliant brethren.

And so the series goes on.   The twelve windows
when complete formed one of the most elaborate
sets of types and antitypes known, and included
not only the life of Christ but eight of His parables
—for some reason a very rare subject in mediæval

glass.   Two panels of the Parable of the Sower—
the seed falling among the thorns and the seed
falling by the wayside—remain, and have been used
to fill up the gaps at the bottom of this window.
Above is a curious subject—the Church with the
three sons of Noah, who hold between them the
world, divided into three regions.   From the MS.
above mentioned we know that this was the type
to the "leaven which a woman took and hid in three
measures of meal till the whole was leavened"—
an idea taken, I think, from St. Augustine.

The subject of Noah and the Ark from the other
window was originally alongside the Baptism of
Christ, the purging of the world by the flood of
waters serving as the type for the purging of the
soul by baptism.

Altogether as one studies these windows one is
almost as much struck by the subtlety of thought
and earnestness of the teaching they embody as by
the glory of their colouring and grace of their
design.

In one of the triforium windows is some glass
which may perhaps be earlier even than this.   It
consists of three medallions, only one of which
is at all perfect, which seem to be part of a life of
St. Alphege, Archbishop of Canterbury, who was

martyred by the Danes. In the one perfect panel which represents the storming of Canterbury by the Danes, the warriors wear the long coats of mail and kite-shaped shields of the Norman period as shown in the Bayeux tapestry, and a ship in one of the other medallions is exactly like those in which William the Conqueror and his knights are there shown crossing the sea. The obscure position of this glass in the triforium is not where one would expect to find a window devoted to St. Alphege, who before the death of Becket was the most important saint that Canterbury could boast; it may be therefore that the medallions have been moved from elsewhere, perhaps from Archbishop Lanfranc's nave, or it may, for all we can tell, be some of Prior Conrad's glass that has survived the fire.

Vendôme. Of other twelfth century work there is not much in existence. There is a Virgin and Child at Vendôme which somewhat recalls Notre Dame de la Belle Verrière but has none of her grace, and I have already referred to the window at Poitiers illustrated in Plate II.

Poitiers. This remarkable and impressive window, which is over 26 feet high and nearly 10 wide, is one of three, and occupies the central light of the

PLATE VI. SCROLL-WORK FROM THE EAST WINDOW, CANTERBURY

Twelfth or early Thirteenth Century

PLATE VII.

BORDER
FROM THE
TRINITY CHAPEL,
CANTERBURY

Twelfth or early
Thirteenth Century

Cathedral apse. The illustration does not show the whole of it, for it is surrounded by a rich border, which in its arrangement of alternate bunches of foliage and knots of interlaced work resembles that of the Jesse Tree at Chartres, and below the Crucifixion is a four-lobed medallion showing the Martyrdom of St. Peter, and the donor offering a model of the window.

The design, as I have said, seems to show that the Byzantine style had lingered on south of the Loire, where no doubt the influence of the Limoges school would be strong, and in view of this fact it is rash to take the age of the Le Mans " Ascension " altogether for granted.

V

EARLY THIRTEENTH CENTURY GLASS
IN ENGLAND

(CANTERBURY AND LINCOLN)

V

EARLY THIRTEENTH CENTURY GLASS IN ENGLAND

(CANTERBURY AND LINCOLN)

IN passing from the twelfth to the thirteenth century one notices a certain loss of the restraint and sense of proportion which gives such dignity and refinement to the earlier work, but on the other hand a certain gain in vivacity and facility of expression. The Greek influence is dying out, but the artists, though with less sense of design than their predecessors, were accomplished at story-telling, in which, however, they seem less serious and more gossiping. Their figures are less tall, and the lines of the drapery from being straight and severe become agitated and flowing.

East of the choir in Canterbury Cathedral is the Trinity Chapel, of which the building was finished in 1185 and to which the body of St. Thomas was

The Trinity Chapel, Canterbury.

translated with great pomp in the year 1220 and
placed in a marvellous jewelled shrine, the position
of which can still be traced on the pavement by
the hollow worn round it by the knees of pilgrims.
All around were gorgeous windows which, with the
exception of those in the little circular chapel at the
east end, known as "Becket's Crown," were filled
with the stories of his posthumous miracles.

It is a little difficult to date these windows.
They cannot of course be earlier than 1185, but I
do not think that any of them are much later
than 1220, though from the fact that one of the
medallions, and one only, contains a representation
of the famous shrine—everywhere else it is the
martyr's tomb in the crypt that is shown—the
particular window containing it cannot have been
executed before the latter date, as the shrine would
not have been in existence.   It may, however, have
been done in that year.   This window and the one
next it seem to me to be by an inferior hand, and
contain certain features not found in the others, but
common in later glass of the thirteenth century.

Whether this represents a gap in the execution
of the windows it is, however, impossible to say
without the evidence of the windows which have
been destroyed.   Seeing that from 1208 to 1213

the country was under an interdict, the existence of such a gap would not be surprising.

None of the windows are entirely filled with their original glass, but four of them are nearly so. The gaps have been filled up with most ingenious imitations of the old glass, executed from 1853 onwards by Mr. Caldwell, under the direction of Mr. G. Austin, and so cleverly are they done that they are very difficult to detect by the eye alone. I do not think that "restoration" of old glass, by which is usually meant filling up or replacing it by imitation of the old work, is ever justifiable, but I am obliged to admit that, if it ever could be so, it has been justified here at Canterbury. I think there is not much doubt that in these four windows, at least, one can see the old glass better for the gaps being filled up with colour than if they had been left white. The principle, however, is a bad one, and I have seen little "restoration" elsewhere that did not disfigure the window.

Fortunately a most indefatigable lover of stained glass, the Rev. J. G. Joyce, has left a series of coloured drawings of the glass as it was in 1841 before restoration. These and his manuscript notes are now in South Kensington Museum, together with some coloured tracings by a Mr. Hudson, and enable us to trace what has been done.   From these we learn that in his time the place of the Crucifixion in the east window was occupied by a figure of the Virgin from a Jesse window, proving that there was once a Jesse window at Canterbury as well as else-where.   Judging from the tracing, the scroll work of the "tree" follows closely the lines of those at Chartres and St. Denis, but is a little more elabo-rate and very beautiful.   It seems to me more in keeping with the earlier than the later work at Canterbury.   Unfortunately no one seems to know what has become of it; but Winston who saw it, quotes it in a lecture as "some of the oldest glass in the country."   If the Cathedral authorities have got it stowed away anywhere I hope they will some day place it in one of the empty windows where it can be seen.

The east window.   This east window, which is in "Becket's Crown," is one of the best preserved, only four or five of its four-and-twenty medallions being new.   It is an example of an arrangement of subjects which occurs also at Bourges and at Chartres, and to which PP. Cahier and Martin in their work on Bourges give the name of "La Nouvelle Alliance." It represents, in fact, the foundation of the Church of Christ, as embodied in His Passion, Resurrection, and Ascension, in the coming of the Holy Ghost, and in the reign of the Son of Man on high, each subject being accompanied and illustrated by "types" from the Old Testament. Here, at Canterbury, on one side of the Crucifixion—which, though new, is doubtless a correct restoration as far as the subject goes—is the sacrifice of the Passover, and on the other is Moses striking the rock in the desert, from whence, as from the side of Christ, gushes the life - giving stream. Above is the sacrifice of Isaac; and below, the spies returning from Eshcol carrying the great cluster of grapes—a type of the wine of the Sacrament.

Above this group come the Entombment (which is reproduced in Plate V.), the Resurrection, the Ascension, the Descent of the Holy Ghost, and Christ in Glory, each with its four types surrounding it. The Resurrection is modern, and so is the Escape of the Spies and the "Majesty." Noah and his Ark is a modern copy of the one in the north choir aisle, but the rest of the panels are original.

The work seems to me fairly early in character, but it is not so well drawn as that in the north choir aisle, and there is not, to me, the same feeling for line in it. It is, however, very beautiful, and the whole window is a shimmer of iridescent colour. Plate VI. shows some of the scroll work that fills the spaces between the medallions.

The Becket windows.
The windows in the Trinity Chapel itself are all devoted to the tale of the posthumous miracles of the Blessed St. Thomas as related in the Chronicle of Prior Benedict, which affords a key to the pictures. The Chronicle is fascinating reading for the homely light it throws upon everyday life in England at the end of the twelfth century. By its means we can trace in the glass the story of the little boy who fell in the Medway while throwing stones at frogs, three of which, very large and green, are shown in the glass; of the workman William, who was overwhelmed by a fall of earth while digging a conduit near Gloucester; of the physician of Perigord and many others, who were one and all restored to life and health through prayer to the Blessed Martyr. There, too, is the tale of Eilward, whose eyes were put out by the magistrate for having, when drunk, broken into the house of Fulk (with whom he had quarrelled over a debt) and taken a pair of hedger's gloves and a whetstone; to whom St. Thomas, who seems to have thought the sentence excessive, appeared in a vision, and with a touch restored his eyesight. Here, too, we see

the awful vengeance of the saint on the knight, Jordan Fitzeisulf, who, when his son was restored to life, meanly neglected to make the offering he had vowed at the Martyr's tomb.

Three of the windows on the north side are fairly perfect, and two on the south side contain many of their original medallions. Of those on the north, one, the sixth from the west, is the best, and might be by the same hand as the east window. An interesting point about it is the border, of which the design is identical with that of a window at Sens which also deals with the history of St. Thomas à Becket. As this window contains the story of Jordan Fitzeisulf, I shall refer to it, if I have to do so again, as the Jordan Fitzeisulf window.

The other two, the fourth and fifth from the west, are, I think, by an inferior hand, and contain, as I have said, certain features not found in the other windows, but common in later glass of the thirteenth century. One of them, the fifth from the west, is divided by the iron-work into four great circles, each of which contains four pear-shaped medallions, their points meeting in the middle. The spandrils between them are filled with scroll work on a ruby ground, not quite so

good as those in the east window; but outside the
large circles—and this is the important point—the
ground is filled in with a regular mosaic of little
pieces forming a repeat pattern as shown in Plate
VIII.   This is the only instance at Canterbury of
this "mosaic diaper," as it is called, which is so
common in glass a little later, and which from the
fact that it could be done "by the yard," and if
necessary by an apprentice, was a much cheaper
method of filling in a background than by scroll
work, which it soon completely superseded.

It is noticeable that it is this window which in
its uppermost medallion contains the representation
already mentioned of the famous shrine, from which
the saint is issuing and addressing a sleeping monk,
who is thought to be the Prior Benedict, the
chronicler of the miracles.

In all the other medallions of the series it is the
tomb of St. Thomas in the crypt, easily recognizable
from the descriptions that remain, at which the
sufferers pay their vows, so that it seems probable
that the window was executed in, or soon after, the
year 1220, in which the saint's body was removed
to the shrine, but while the memory of the tomb
in the crypt was still fresh.

The other, the fourth from the west, has a very

PLATE VIII.   BORDER AND MOSAIC DIAPER, FROM THE TRINITY CHAPEL,
CANTERBURY
Thirteenth Century

remarkable peculiarity, very seldom met with in glass of the Early Period at all. The blue background to the figures in the medallions, which is of a paler and poorer quality than in the other windows, is covered all over with a thin " matt " of enamel, from which a delicate diaper pattern has been scratched out. Presumably the artist had for some reason been unable to get any more of the splendid deep blue glass, and used this means to give richness and texture to his background. The only other thirteenth century glass I know of in which at all the same thing has been done is at St. Urbain at Troyes, but that belongs, I believe, to quite the latter part of the century. It was a common device in the fourteenth century, but the patterns used then were of quite a different character.

Except for the grisaille windows at York and Lincoln. Salisbury, the only other extensive remains of thirteenth century work in England are those in Lincoln Cathedral, which, however, are little more than wreckage, and consequently very difficult to date with any attempt at precision. The only window in which any of the glass is in its original position is the great rose window in the north transept, and even this, though the original design can still be made out, is much mutilated.

The lancets under the rose in the south transept and the east windows of the choir aisles contain a miscellaneous collection of medallions, separated from their surrounding ornament and glazed in with remains of thirteenth century grisaille.   Other medallions, too, have been used to fill gaps in the north rose, and the south rose is filled, with the exception of one light which retains its original fourteenth century foliage pattern, with scraps of thirteenth century ornament of which the effect, with the sunlight twinkling through, is wonderfully beautiful.

The medallions are not, I think, all of one date, which is not surprising, for the filling of the windows of a big cathedral must always have taken many years.   The difficulty of dating them is increased by the fact that much of the painting does not seem to have been so well "fired" as at Canterbury, and in many cases has perished altogether.   This seems to have happened in recent years, for Mr. Westlake shows many details in his drawings of the glass which I cannot now distinguish.   Where the painting remains we find that in a few of the medallions the drapery is drawn in the stiff manner of the twelfth and very early thirteenth century, but in most of them the later more flowing treatment prevails. In some, too, the blue of the backgrounds resembles that used at Canterbury, but in many, and notably in the north rose, it is of a purplish colour and much less agreeable. In a few it is of quite a grey blue.

Nowhere can I trace the same hand as at Canterbury, and the borders and ornament are quite different; but that the artist had access to some at least of the same designs is shown by a medallion in the south choir aisle which represents Noah receiving the Dove, and is practically a replica of the Canterbury one in Plate IV., with a boat-like hull added to the Ark. It is not, however, nearly so good. According to Mr. Westlake the work at Lincoln strongly resembles that at Bourges, and to me it has something in common with that in the Sainte Chapelle at Paris.

Lincoln Cathedral was not finished till after St. Hugh's death in 1199, so none of the glass can be older than that. On the whole, I think the bulk of the glass is a little later than any but the very last of the work at Canterbury, that it is by a different hand, and shows less taste both in colour and design. Probably it was done between 1220 and 1240.

I am confirmed in this view by the examination

The south
rose

of the fragments which fill the great south rose, which consist entirely of thirteenth century ornament and most probably once formed the setting of these same medallions. A little of it is scroll work, but the greater part is "mosaic diaper" of the kind shown in Plate VIII., and which is so characteristic of French work after 1220, whereas we only find it beginning at Canterbury.

Some of the medallions are, however, very interesting, the best being those in which the drapery shows the earlier treatment. In the north choir aisle is a good one of the Israelites crossing a Red Sea of a fine streaky ruby, and in the south choir aisle is one of St. Thomas à Becket being conducted to Heaven by angels and carrying the damaged top of his head in his hands. By a touch of realism both parts of his head have been made of glass that has slight ruby streaks in it, giving it a gory appearance. This is the earliest example I know of the deliberate use of an accident of colouring in the glass to produce a realistic effect.

Among the medallions which have been glazed into the north rose is one representing the funeral of St. Hugh of Lincoln in 1199, the coffin being carried by three archbishops and three kings.

One of the kings was William of Scotland, and the other King John of England (the only occasion on which I know of that monarch appearing in a pleasant light), but the artist must have put the third king in for the sake of symmetry as there is no record of his presence.

A curious medallion in the south transept shows Salome dancing before Herod, not in the languorous Oriental fashion one would have expected of her, but turning a somersault worthy of the music-hall stage, with a lavish display of red stockings. A similar treatment of the subject occurs at Bourges, and also in sculpture over one of the west doors at Rouen Cathedral.

The north rose still retains about three-quarters The north of its original glazing, and enables one to make out rose. the design. In the centre is Christ, and in the four petal-like lights which surround Him are, or were, figures of the Blessed seated, not in circles but in horizontal rows. Filling the spandrils between these lights are four trefoils, of which two still each contain an angel swinging a censer, in an attitude ingeniously fitted to the shape of the light. Outside these, sixteen circular lights form a ring round the whole, and once represented the Second Coming of Christ. At the top is Christ seated on the rainbow, and in two lights on either side of Him are angels carrying instruments of the Passion. Next come St. Peter and the other Apostles, six in one light on each side, and below them, in the lights level with the centre, are the four archangels sounding trumpets. The lower half of the circle was probably devoted to the resurrection of the dead and perhaps their judgment, but of these only one light remains, showing the dead rising from their graves, the rest being filled with single figures from elsewhere.

The spandrils between these circles are filled with little triangular lights forming an inner and an outer ring of sixteen each. Of these the inner ring is filled with white wavy pointed stars on a red ground and the outer with similar red stars on a dark blue ground, thus suggesting the idea—in *colour* alone, without use of light or shade, of light and warmth radiating from the centre.[1]

---

[1] Were it not for the difference in the source of the light one would be reminded of Kipling's lines :—

" The first are white with the heat of Hell and the second are red with pain,"

and

" . . . Tomlinson looked up and up, and saw against the night
The belly of a tortured star blood-red in Hellmouth light ;
And Tomlinson looked down and down, and saw beneath his feet
The frontlet of a tortured star milk-white in Hellmouth heat."

According to Mr. Westlake the central Christ has no stigmata, while the one in the outer circle has them ; but the painting has now perished too much for me to see this even at close quarters. His theory is that the centre represents Christ as "The Word,—the uncreated Wisdom, as Creator, resting,"—and the outer circle shows His last coming as Judge.

VI

THIRTEENTH CENTURY GLASS IN FRANCE

(SENS AND CHARTRES)

VI

THIRTEENTH CENTURY GLASS
IN FRANCE

(SENS AND CHARTRES)

IT was at Sens that Thomas à Becket took refuge Sens. during his exile. His mitre and chasuble are still preserved there, and the connection between the two places seems to have remained very intimate.

It will be remembered that William of Sens was the first architect of the choir of Canterbury, and it is not surprising to find the resemblance between the cathedrals at the two places very marked indeed. Not only does one at once perceive the same hand in the architecture, but what remains of the early glass at Sens is quite incontestably the work of the same artist who gave us the east window and the Jordan Fitzeisulf window at Canterbury.

There are four of these windows at Sens, all in

87

The Good
Samaritan.
the north choir aisle. They have suffered a little
from restoration but not very much. Their subjects
respectively from left to right are, the Life and Death
of St. Thomas à Becket, the Story of St. Eustace,
the Parable of the Prodigal Son, and the Parable of
the Good Samaritan. This last is another "type
and antitype" window, and corresponds exactly in
the arrangement of its subjects with one of the lost
windows in the choir of Canterbury as described in
the manuscript catalogue before mentioned. The
verses, however, which were in the Canterbury
window are omitted at Sens. To the mediæval mind
the parable of the Good Samaritan was much more
than a mere illustration of "neighbourliness." To
them the "man who went down from Jerusalem"
—the City of God—"to Jericho," was Adam
leaving Paradise, the thieves were the seven deadly
sins, the Priest and the Levite were the law of
Moses, and the Good Samaritan was Christ Himself.
It is this reading of the subject which is here
illustrated. From the fact that at Sens it is
isolated, while at Canterbury it was, as we have
seen, one of a series, I think we may conclude that
Sens is the later of the two. The drawing of the
medallions resembles that of the older work at
Canterbury, whereas the setting of them is a little

later in character, showing the beginnings of "mosaic diaper." It seems to me probable, therefore, that for the subjects the actual drawings from Canterbury were used in a fresh setting. We know from the Treatise of Theophilus that designs for windows at this time were drawn out in full size on whitened boards, which also served apparently as the bench on which the window was put together. Not much would be left of the drawing when the window was finished, and the bench would be re-whitewashed for the next window; but from the fact that similar treatments of the same subject repeatedly occur, it seems to me not unlikely that drawings of figure subjects for medallions were kept on separate sheets of parchment, or in a book, and used again.

To the scene of the Good Samaritan rescuing the traveller there are four scenes showing as a "type" the Passion of Christ. Of these the Crucifixion is treated in the most striking and original way, which I rather think occurs also at Bourges. On one side of the cross stands a female figure wearing a crown and with a nimbus, and receiving in a chalice the blood which flows from the side of Christ; on the other, a six-winged seraph is sheathing a sword. The latter is, no doubt, a symbol of the peace made between God and man by the atonement on the Cross,—I think PP. Cahier and Martin identify him with the angel that guarded the gates of Paradise,—while the crowned female figure is, of course, the Church.

The Prodigal
Son.

The next window, containing the Parable of the Prodigal Son, differs from the others in having straight iron-work and a more formal arrangement of the medallions. I do not think, however, that it is older. One charming panel in it is a good illustration of the attitude of the artists of that day on the question of colour. The Prodigal Son is feeding pigs, of which one is white, two blue, one green, and one red! The next scene shows him making his way homeward, undeterred by the efforts to hamper him of several devils as gaily and variously coloured as the pigs. There is considerable dramatic power shown in this figure of the Prodigal. Let no one call the drawing of this period *bad* drawing. It would be as true to call Japanese drawing "bad." It is drawing in a convention—a convention different from our own, but which, once mastered, set the artist free to express action and emotion without being further hampered by technical difficulties.

Of the other two, the one dealing with the story of St. Thomas à Becket is the one which most reminds me of Canterbury. Here there is no doubt that we have the same hand that gave us the Jordan Fitzeisulf window there. The border is identical,—an unusual thing at that time even in the same church,—and the representation of Becket's tomb in the crypt is precisely the same. The Becket. window.

I am less certain about the St. Eustace window. Its general effect is very different from the others, being flatter and less sparkling; but this may be due to the work of a restorer. The figures, however, do not fit and decorate the medallions as well as in the other windows or in those at Canterbury; in many cases part of a figure has to project into the border.[1] The medallions themselves, too, are of rather awkward shapes, and the design of the iron-work not very restful. The scroll work, however, is very like that in the east window at Canterbury—so like that one can hardly doubt their common origin. It may be that here, too, the artist has used some one else's figure designs, less successfully than in the Good Samaritan window. The story of St. Eustace.

There is a Life of St. Eustace at Chartres in

[1] This is a later feature, and found at Bourges and elsewhere.

which the scenes bear a general resemblance to those at Sens, but decorate their spaces much better.

To sum up, I think that these windows at Sens, with the possible exception of the Life of St. Eustace, are the work of the same artist as the Jordan Fitzeisulf window and the east window in "Becket's Crown" at Canterbury; that in the Good Samaritan window he was using the cartoons of his master, who designed the windows in Canterbury choir, of which two, as we have seen, remain. He may have come from Canterbury at the time of the interdict in King John's reign (1208–1213), when all work there must have been suspended, and not returned, leaving another to finish the work after the interdict was removed. It would be a very probable date for the Sens work, but in the absence of the destroyed windows at Canterbury it is pure conjecture.

Chartres. Meanwhile, ever since the fire in 1194, the people of Chartres, careless of their personal losses, had been working in a flame of enthusiasm and devotion at the rebuilding of their Cathedral. Every one, nobles, merchants, craftsmen, and peasants, gave what they could. Some gave money, some materials, some provisions for the workmen. Those who had nothing else gave their labour, even

PLATE IX.   WESTERN LANCETS AND ROSE, CHARTRES CATHEDRAL
Twelfth and Thirteenth Century

harnessing themselves to carts to drag stone for the building. Heaven itself seemed to lend its aid, for it is said that Our Lady worked many miracles of healing at her shrine at Chartres, which soon became a thirteenth century Lourdes, to which pilgrims came from all countries, leaving offerings of money or jewels.

Finally, in 1210 the main part of the building seems to have been finished. " Entirely rebuilt in hewn stone," says William le Breton some years later, " the Cathedral of Chartres has nothing to fear from temporal fire from now till the day of judgment, and will save from eternal fire the many Christians who by their alms have contributed to its reconstruction."

The great church was now ready to receive its decoration : The altars, the painting, the sculpture were still to be done, and above all the one hundred and twenty-five great windows, with the three great roses, and forty-seven lesser ones had to be filled with the glass which still makes Chartres Cathedral one of the wonders of the world. In the year 1226 Saint Louis came to the throne. Eight years later he acquired the Comté of Chartres, and lent his powerful aid to the work, giving the great rose window in the north transept and the five

lancets below it, as well as other windows. The
King of Castile gave a window too, and following
these royal donors a crowd of princes, seigneurs,
and churchmen added their gifts, while forty-seven
windows were given by the Guilds of Chartres alone.
Yet even so it was thirty years more before the
bulk of the work was completed, and the actual
consecration did not take place, for some reason,
till October 17, 1260, when it was performed with
great pomp and rejoicing before Saint Louis and
his family and an immense concourse of prelates,
nobles, and common people.

There is nothing in the world quite like the
Cathedral of Chartres. In the quality of its work
Canterbury is as good or even better, but for the
proper appreciation of the glass of the twelfth and
thirteenth centuries it is necessary to have *every*
window of the building filled with it in order that
the eye may get used to the gloom and attuned to
the pitch of the colour ; and it is only at Chartres
that this is even approximately the case. I know
nothing like the effect on one of several hours
spent in the building, the awe and wonder, mingled
with a strange sort of exaltation, which it produces.

Even when its windows were complete, Canterbury can hardly have had quite the same effect, for

its clerestory is much smaller, and it has not the splendid width of nave and choir which enables one to see the great clerestory windows of Chartres so well.   In the thirteenth century the nave at Canterbury was still the old Norman nave of Lanfranc, of which the windows were, as an old drawing shows, comparatively small ; nor indeed do we know for certain if they had coloured glass in them.

York is almost as complete as Chartres, but the glass there is nearly all of the fourteenth and fifteenth centuries, and though it is in a sense quite as beautiful, with all its great windows twinkling with lovely colour, yet the subjects are too small to be seen from below, and there is nothing like the awe-inspiring majesty of the ranks of colossal saints which fill the clerestory of Chartres.

That the master or masters of Canterbury and Sens came to Chartres is, I think, certain ; the Canterbury tradition is traceable in so much of the work.   Here I imagine he or they ended their life's work, leaving their pupils and their pupils' successors to carry it on in the later style which they developed as they went along.   One of these, no doubt, was that Clement of Chartres who signed his name in the window at Rouen which Mr. Saint has sketched in Plate XIV. I think I can trace his hand in some of the windows on the south side of the nave at Chartres, in the treatment of the mosaic diaper in which various shades of blue have been so skilfully blended as to produce, as at Rouen, a lovely play and ripple of colour over the whole surface of the window.

Perhaps the most notable development of the style at Chartres is the increase in the use of mosaic diaper, of the kind illustrated in Plate VIII., as a setting for the medallions, instead of the leafy scroll work formerly used.

At Canterbury the mosaic diaper setting is the exception, only occurring in one window; at Sens it is introduced tentatively, but at Chartres it is the rule. The scroll-work filling only occurs, I think, in three windows of the lower tier. One of these is the St. Eustace window already mentioned, which to me is strongly reminiscent of Canterbury work—more so, indeed, as far as the medallions go, than the similar one at Sens.

The four extremities.
It is only at the four extremities of the Cathedral at Chartres that we find any connected idea governing the choice of subjects. The three twelfth century windows were already, as I have said, devoted to the ancestry and life of Christ,

PLATE X. THE BIG ANGEL.   PLATE XI. DAVID

FROM THE CLERESTORY OF THE APSE, CHARTRES CATHEDRAL
Thirteenth Century

PLATE XII. AMAURY DE MONTFORT, FROM THE CHOIR CLERESTORY,
CHARTRES CATHEDRAL

Thirteenth Century

and the thirteenth century rose window above them shows His second coming. The seven great lancets of the apse are given up to the glorification of the Virgin, the especial patroness of Chartres. The north rose and the lights below it seem to show the human ancestry of Christ culminating in Saint Anne and the Virgin, while opposite in the south transept is the Christ of the Apocalypse.

In other parts of the church the choice of theme seems to have been left to the taste of the donors, subject only to the general arrangement of medallion windows in the lower tier and huge single figures in the clerestory lights. Thus in the lower windows we find the story of Noah next to that of St. Lubin, Bishop of Chartres ; the story of St. Eustace next that of Joseph.

One or two of the clerestory windows are medallion windows, the medallions being on a very large scale, but most of them are filled, as I say, with single figures of saints, nearly twice life-size. So large are they that their faces have had to be composed of several pieces of glass. A brownish pink is used for the flesh, and the eyes are separate pieces of white with the pupil painted in. As the flesh colour has in many cases darkened considerably from the effects of time and weather,

7

the effect of the brilliant whites of the eyes is somewhat weird and startling.

Here again there seems to be no special idea governing the order of subjects, which were probably left to the donors, who would choose their patron saints.

The Guild windows.

It is at Chartres that for the first time, as I believe, the donors of the windows are made much account of in the glass. It is true that at St. Denis there are two very tiny figures of Abbot Suger,—in one case, prostrate, in simple monk's dress, at the feet of the Virgin in the Annunciation, and in the other, holding up a model of the Jesse window,—and there is a donor at Poitiers, but at Canterbury and Sens there is nothing to show by whom the windows were given. At Chartres, however, it is far otherwise. Partly, perhaps, because of the emulation that had been shown in presenting windows, nearly every one contains some record of its donor. In the case of those given by the Guilds this takes the form of a little panel introduced into the bottom of the window, showing members of the Guild at work—bakers, butchers, tanners, furriers, money-changers and so on— charming and valuable little pictures of the everyday life of the time. More noble donors are represented by their portraits, either kneeling at the foot of the window or, as in the clerestory of the choir, where the rose-lights of the tracery are filled with a splendid series of princes and nobles armed and on horseback, each recognizable by his shield and banner.

The one illustrated in Mr. Saint's sketch in Plate XII. is Amaury de Montfort, brother of our own Simon de Montfort who led the rebellion of the barons against Henry III., and son of that Simon de Montfort who led the crusade against the Albigenses and was made Lord of Languedoc for his pains.   Amaury, who succeeded him in 1218, finding himself not strong enough to hold the country, had ceded his rights six years later to the King of France, and was made in return Constable of France.

Amaury de Montfort.

The great rose window of the south transept and the lancets below it are the gift of Pierre Mauclerc, Count of Dreux and Duke of Brittany. His arms are in the trefoils of the rose and in the central lancet.   At the foot of the lancets on either side are portraits of himself, his wife, Alix de Thouars, and his son and daughter, all kneeling. From the fact that his wife died in 1226 it has been argued that the window must have been

Pierre Mauclerc.

executed, or at least designed, before that date. I do not know that the argument is absolutely conclusive, but the fact seems probable. The window, however, cannot be many years older than this date. The choir would almost certainly be the first part of the church to be glazed, and the windows in the clerestory there were certainly not finished till after 1220. One, indeed, has the figure of a king of France on horseback as donor, who has always been called St. Louis. It is, however, quite possible, as far as I can see, that the figure is his father, Louis VIII., or even Philip Augustus, who died in 1223, for he bears the lilies of France only, without the castle of Castile.

St. Louis.   Assuming therefore that the date of the south rose is shortly before 1226, then Pierre Mauclerc, at the time he gave this and the other windows in the church which bear his arms, was practically an independent sovereign. When St. Louis ascended the throne as a boy in 1226, under the Regency of his mother, the wise and beautiful, if somewhat imperious, Blanche of Castile, Pierre Mauclerc, in company with Thibault of Champagne, who was Count of Chartres, and many other barons of France, took up arms against his sovereign, scorning to acknowledge the overlordship of a boy and a woman. Eight years later the boy and the woman, aided by the devoted support of the Commons, had brought them all to submission, and Thibault had yielded up Chartres to the Crown. It seems to me not unlikely that this latter event is marked by the gift of the north rose and the lancets below, which contain St. Louis's own arms and those of his mother. If so, the glass of Chartres may be considered as a landmark in the history of the growth of France into a nation. Whether this is so or not, the north rose cannot in any case be earlier than 1226, the year of St. Louis's accession.

This north rose, or Rose of France as it is called, has in its centre light the Virgin with the Child, in a purple tunic with a blue robe and nimbus against a ground of rich ruby. In the twelve radiating lights round her are : above her head, four doves ; on her right and left, four angels,—two on either side,—two incensing and two holding candles ; and below, four six-winged seraphs. Outside these are twelve kings of Judah, the Virgin's ancestors, and outside these again is a ring of the Prophets who foretold Christ's coming. Below, in the five great lancets, is a huge figure of Saint Anne carrying the infant Virgin, having on her right King

The north rose and lancets.

David and on her left Solomon, and beyond these
Melchizedek and Aaron, types of Christ as King
and High Priest.   Below St. Anne is a great shield
with the arms of St. Louis, but under each of the
four other figures is a kind of " predella," in which
are shown, as a contrast : below David, Saul falling on
his sword ; below Solomon, Jeroboam worshipping
the golden calves ; below Melchizedek, Nebuchad-
nezzar ; and below Aaron, Pharaoh being whirled
away, horse and man, in the Red Sea.   In this last
scene the artist has been in a dilemma.   The backgrounds of these lancets are alternately red and
blue, and Pharaoh's should have been blue, but it
represents the *Red* Sea, and the artist has had to
get out of the difficulty by making it a kind of
maroon purple.

The south
rose and
lancets.

The idea of the window is the same as that of
the Jesse Tree : Humanity preparing, through the
ages, for the coming of Christ, and culminating in
His Mother.   The rose and lancets opposite show
the fulfilment.   Here Christ is seen enthroned in
the centre of the rose, as St. John beheld Him,
surrounded by angels and by the four great beasts,
and by the four-and-twenty elders seated on their
thrones, in a double ring round the whole.

In the five lancets below are, in the centre,

the Virgin and Child, and on either side the four Evangelists, borne, by a quaint conceit, like children on the strong shoulders of the major Prophets. The general arrangement of the windows is the same, but the detail seems to me to bear out the supposition that the southern rose is by some years the earlier of the two.   In both windows the outer and the inner ring of figures are contained in circular medallions, but where in the south rose the "filling in" is done by means of scroll work, in the north transept "mosaic diaper" is everywhere used. The borders of the lancets, too, are of an older type, and more beautiful in the south transept than in the north.

Both, however, are very lovely, and the more I look at them the more I admire the nameless workers who could so use red and blue—such difficult colours to combine well. For red and blue are everywhere the groundwork of the colour scheme—green, purple, brown, and yellow being only used in small quantities to relieve them. It must be remembered, too, that the artist *could never see the effect of his work till it was finished.* Nowadays the stained-glass painter can put his work together temporarily by fastening it with bees-wax to a large sheet of white glass, and can work

on it so ; but the artist of the twelfth and thirteenth
centuries, as we know from Theophilus, and as was
probably the case for long after, did all his work
"on the bench." The most he could do would be
to hold a few pieces together in his hands up to
the light, but for the rest he had to trust to his
experience and training.

Not quite always did he succeed. Much
depended upon his getting just the right quality
of blue, and sometimes this seems to have failed
him. I have already noticed the rather purplish
blue which is found in some of the windows at
Lincoln, and this occurs again at Chartres in the
central lancet of the apse, and the one next it on
the north containing the big angel illustrated in
Plate X. This purplish blue when interspersed
with red produces at a distance the effect of
a rather unpleasant mauve, making these two
windows less attractive in colour than the others.
This purplish blue occurs again in the north rose
of Notre Dame at Paris, but there the artist has
countered it by the use of a good deal of a rather
sharp pale green, which completely balances it and
turns the window into perhaps the most glorious
of all the great rose windows of France.

The apse.   Five of the seven great lancets of the clerestory

of the apse are devoted to the glorification of the
Virgin Mother, or perhaps one should say, to
the fact of the Virgin Birth. This is what one
would expect at Chartres. Not only is the church
dedicated to Notre Dame, but the place in the
Middle Ages was held sacred to her above all
others in France.

Tradition says that the Church occupies the site
of a grotto in which the Druids worshipped "the
Virgin that shall bear a child," of whom they had
set up a wooden image, which was preserved by
the Christians when the grotto became a Christian
church. Certain it is that down to the Revolution
a very ancient and quite black wooden statue was
worshipped in the Chapel of Notre Dame Sous-
terre—the ancient grotto—where it had been at
all events since the days of Fulbert, who built
the eleventh century Cathedral. The Sansculottes
burnt it, and its place has been taken by a modern
work which professes to be a copy of it.

Chartres, too, can boast of the possession of
the Holy Veil. Given to Charlemagne by the
Byzantine Emperor, Constantine Porphyrogenitus,
it has escaped successive fires, and though cut in
two at the Revolution, is still preserved in the
Treasury.

Owing to the great height and narrowness of the lancets, each contains several figures or figure subjects, one above the other. In the head of the central lancet is Our Lady enthroned, with her Child on her knee, and below her are the Annunciation and the Salutation. In the head of the light on either side is an angel incensing, and in the lights beyond these, a cherub and a seraph. Below these are Moses, Aaron,[1] David, and the four major Prophets— Isaiah, Jeremiah, Ezekiel—and Daniel. The arrangement of these figures seems, however, quite haphazard, and as if the original design had not been carried out. The two remaining lancets, on the extreme right and left, contain, respectively, scenes from the lives of St. John the Baptist and St. Peter. How far these are meant to have a bearing on the central subject I am not quite sure. The uppermost subjects in them are the Baptism of Christ and the " Domine, quo vadis ? "

The big angel. The Big Angel (Plate X.) on the north side of the Virgin is especially puzzling. The other six lights of the apse have each three figures or figure subjects, set one above the other in elongated medallions,—Plate XI. shows two of them, King

---

[1] The miraculous budding of Aaron's rod was considered a type of the Virgin Birth.

David and Ezekiel,—and at the foot of each is a panel showing the donors. The other figures are so set as to form regular tiers round the apse, but this angel is twice the size of any of them and forces the figure below—Aaron—down out of line, leaving no room for another figure between him and the donor.

Perhaps this light represents part of a design for the apse which was afterwards modified in order to get more figures in. The donor is one Gaufridus, who has been identified with a certain Godfrey d'Illiers, a gentleman of the neighbourhood, whereas the rest are given by the Guilds — the bakers, butchers, money - changers, and furriers, which latter are seen actually bringing their window.

The Prophets bear a good deal of resemblance to the figures from the clerestory at Canterbury. The Isaiah at both places wears the same curious head-dress—a little round hat, not unlike the latest form of " bowler " of our own days. The figures are not from the same drawings, for the attitudes are different, but the Chartres artist has at least remembered Canterbury choir, which was probably the work of his master, thirty or forty years earlier.

Notice the simple architectural canopy over this The canopy. angel. All the single figures at Chartres and in most other thirteenth century windows have them, and their counterparts may be found in the canopies over the sculptured figures on the porches outside. They occur also at Canterbury over some of the surviving figures from the clerestory, but it is noteworthy that whereas at Canterbury the canopies are round arched (and the same is true of the architecture in the medallion windows), at Chartres they are nearly all either cusped or pointed, which I take as additional evidence in support of my opinion that the Canterbury work is the older of the two.

In thirteenth century work these canopies are a fairly unobtrusive feature, but in the next period they were destined, as we shall see later, to be developed out of all reason or proportion.

VII

OTHER THIRTEENTH CENTURY WINDOWS

VII

OTHER THIRTEENTH CENTURY WINDOWS

A SINGLE band of craftsmen might, as far as we Salisbury and Peterborough. can now tell, have been responsible for nearly all the stained glass that was produced at any one time in the twelfth century in England and the north of France ; but by the time the Trinity Chapel at Canterbury was finished, a great many such bands must have been at work, yet all deriving their art from the same source—the school of Chartres, St. Denis, and Canterbury. The output was enormous, especially in the first half of the thirteenth century. I have already spoken of Lincoln, but Salisbury and Peterborough were once rich in glass of the thirteenth century, that of Peterborough—now destroyed—being known to have been given, some of it at least, as early as 1214, and York has the famous " Five Sisters."

Bourges.   In France, Bourges is only second to Chartres for the quantity and interest of its early glass, which was certainly begun long before the windows of Chartres were finished.   Every one knows the rose windows of Notre Dame at Paris, and besides these Amiens, Beauvais, Laon, Rheims, Tours, Soissons, Auxerre, and in fact nearly all the great cathedrals of France, contain glass of the period, while fragments of it are to be found in many parish churches both in England and France.

Westwell.   At Westwell in Kent, for instance, is a Jesse Tree of 1240–1250 which is well worth study, in which the details of the foliage resemble fragments of one at Salisbury and another at Troyes, and show the development that had taken place from the Jesse Trees of Chartres and St. Denis.

It is impossible, however, in the limits of this work to describe even all the important windows of this period, and I have taken those I have already described as typical of their time and as together showing the progress of the development of the art.

The Sainte Chapelle.   The most complete example of the work of the latter part of the thirteenth century is the Sainte Chapelle in Paris, built by St. Louis to contain the Crown of Thorns, which he had purchased with

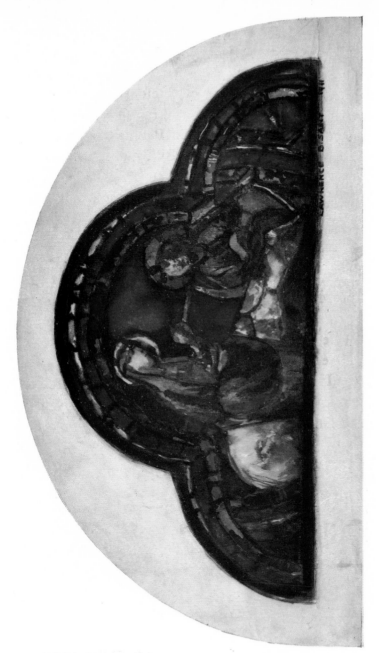

PLATE XIII. THE FLIGHT INTO EGYPT, FROM THE SOUTH AISLE, CHARTRES CATHEDRAL
Thirteenth Century

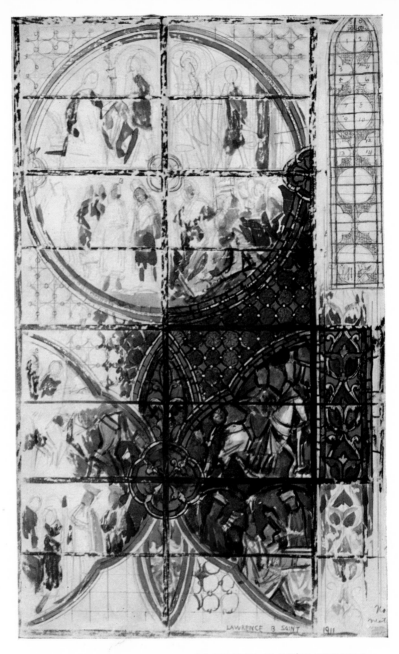

PLATE XIV. WORK OF CLEMENT OF CHARTRES, IN ROUEN CATHEDRAL
Late Thirteenth Century

other relics from the Emperor of Constantinople, who was then in need of ready money. The Chapel was consecrated in 1248, but although some at least of the windows are said to have been prepared beforehand and to have been in their place on that occasion, yet the series was certainly not completed till after the death of St. Louis in 1270, as that event is represented in one of them.

The glass has unfortunately suffered a good deal from restoration, and it is difficult now to say quite how much beauty it once had, but it must be confessed that at present it gives one none of the joy and wonder of Chartres. Yet the very design of the Chapel shows the importance which the art had now attained, for the building is constructed entirely with a view to being filled with stained glass, being in fact a mere glass-house with no wall spaces at all. If the colour effect may be judged of from the specimens of the original glass now in South Kensington Museum, the place must have been a wondrous Aladdin's cave of jewels, but at the same time it may be doubted whether the arrangement was a wise one. The windows at Chartres gain immensely by the spaces of gloom between them, whereas here the eye gets no rest.

In detail, apart from colour, the work shows a

8

certain falling off.   The artist seems to have been cramped by the necessity of adapting the medallion window to such narrow lights.   One misses the fine broad border which does so much to "pull together" the earlier medallion windows.   The borders at the Sainte Chapelle are narrow and uninteresting, and even so the medallions have sometimes to overlap them.

Work of Clement of Chartres at Rouen.

On the other hand, the work of Clement of Chartres in Rouen Cathedral, which is as late as 1290–1295, is as good as anything that was done in the thirteenth century.   Besides a great many broken remains of thirteenth century work in the nave, there are five complete windows in the ambulatory of the apse.   Two of these between them illustrate the story of Joseph, and are particularly beautiful.   One of them (Plate XIV.) is signed by Clement of Chartres, and the other is obviously by the same hand.   I should hesitate, however, to say positively that the other three are his work too, but I think two of them may be.   Of these, one contains in its lowest section the story of the Good Samaritan, with other subjects above which I have not identified, and the other—a very good one—the story of St. Julian, which is a parallel to that of Œdipus except that, being Christian, it ends with atonement and forgiveness.

The fifth window illustrates the Passion, Re-surrection, and Ascension of Christ. It is hardly as good as the others, and is very red and hot in general colour. The filling in, of yellow suns on a blue ground, is very unlike any other thirteenth century work. On the whole this window seems to me to show a certain restlessness, indicative of the change of style that was so soon to follow. The redness, however, may perhaps be intentional, as being appropriate to the subject, for of the three twelfth century windows in the west end of Chartres Cathedral, the one which illustrates the Passion is far redder than the others.

The iron-work of these windows shows a return to the straight-bar system, but the relation of the medallions to the iron-work is, as may be seen by the illustration, wholly different to what it was in the twelfth century. By the end of the thirteenth century the bent iron-work has wholly disappeared.

Before leaving the Early Period I must touch upon another of its developments, namely, the grisaille window.

Side by side with the richly coloured windows which we have been considering, there had grown up during the thirteenth century a style of window in which a wholly different effect was aimed at. Grisaille windows.

These are what are called grisaille windows, in which the bulk of the glass is white, only studded here and there with jewels of colour and with, perhaps, a coloured border, the surface of the white glass being variegated and ornamented with delicate patterns in painted line work. The effect of this in old glass is very beautiful,—there are few things lovelier than "the Five Sisters" at York,—but all modern attempts to imitate it have been hopeless failures, looking like so much transparent paper. Perhaps our modern white glass is too clear and hard-looking, or the difference may be merely that between the work of those who are artists and those who are not.

The causes which led to the development of this style of window were probably two : one, the desire for more light, of which the richly coloured windows admitted but little ; and the other, simply economy, for a window of this sort could be produced comparatively cheaply. Then, too, the Cistercians, whose rule, adopted in the twelfth century, prohibited the use of colour altogether, had shown what could be done in patterns of white glass and lead alone.

Unless you count the "gryphon windows" in St. Denis, which are mainly the work of Viollet-le-

Duc, grisaille seems almost wholly a development of the thirteenth century. It is interesting to see that just as the design of the coloured window seems always to have been conceived as a light pattern on a dark ground, so the earliest grisaille, even though the quantity of white far exceeds the colour, still seems to have been conceived as a white pattern on a coloured ground, the ground being, as it were, almost entirely hidden by the pattern. Later this idea gets reversed, and the coloured pieces are mere jewels or lines contained in the pattern.

In a white window the leads, from their greater thickness, are more conspicuous than the traced lines of the painting, and in consequence it is upon the leads that the artist depends for the main features of his design. The earliest grisaille windows may be divided into two classes: those in which the pattern is formed of narrow "straps" of white glass interlacing or seeming to interlace; and the other in which the leads form a flat geometrical pattern, as at Lincoln. The painted pattern on the glass consists of branching scroll work in simple outline, forming stems and the round-lobed leaves which were the thirteenth century convention for foliage. In the earlier work the ground is covered with delicate cross-hatching, which at a distance resolves itself into a pearly grey, against which the scroll work stands out white. At first, too, the painted pattern is, so to speak, contained within the leading, and merely enriches and emphasizes the pattern formed by it; but in later work, towards the end of the century, it becomes independent of the leading and grows through it, spreading over the surface of the window in graceful curves like a creeper over a trellis. The influence of the medallion window is often seen in contemporary grisaille, of which the design frequently consists of interlacing medallions of strap-work of the same shape as those in the coloured windows.

Rheims.

The ornament surrounding some of the figures in the triforium of St. Remi at Rheims, and which Mr. Westlake considers to date from about 1200, contains so much colour as to be hardly grisaille, and the same may be said of one of the lancets in the north transept of Lincoln Cathedral, of which the others contain grisaille of a later date. There is, however, some very early thirteenth century grisaille—true grisaille, with interlacing bands—at St. Serge at Angers, and some at Soissons of about 1230. Chartres has four or five grisaille windows, of the middle of the century or a little

Angers, Soissons, and Chartres.

earlier, in the apsidal chapels. These have broad, richly coloured borders, a very beautiful feature, which one finds also at Salisbury.

According to Professor Lethaby[1] the original glazing of Westminster Abbey, begun in 1253, was, at least in the lower windows, of grisaille, of which some remains are in the triforium. From the fabric rolls we know the name of the master-glazier, Lawrence, presumably an Englishman, and the weekly accounts show wages paid to fourteen glaziers in all. *Westminster Abbey.*

The few remains of old glass which that eighteenth century vandal, the architect Wyatt, has left us at Salisbury include some very beautiful and interesting specimens of thirteenth century grisaille, of which the date is, according to Winston, from 1240 to 1270. In most of these the pattern when analysed is found to be formed of over-lapping (not interlacing) geometrical forms out-lined in bands of colour and filled in with white, painted with patterns of the usual conventional scroll work on a cross-hatched ground. There are besides, however, some remains of ornamental glazing of an interesting and rare kind in which there is no painting whatever, and the pattern *Salisbury.*

[1] " *Westminster Abbey and the Kings' Craftsmen.*"

is obtained by lead-work alone, forming diagonal white bands interlacing in various ways on a white ground, and containing here and there between them little square dies of blue. Some coloured tracings of these may be seen in South Kensington Museum.

"The Five Sisters" of York.
The finest grisaille windows in England or, for that matter, in the world, are the five immense lancets which fill the end of the north transept of York Minster and are known as "the Five Sisters." Their date is probably about 1260. The iron-work in them is straight-barred, and the massive main bars, placed every $3\frac{1}{2}$ feet or so, divide the space between the broad borders into a succession of squares, one above the other, each one of which is occupied by a medallion—a different shape in each light—outlined with a narrow band of colour, and having bosses of colour at the centre and between the medallions. One hardly can trace the plan of the painted pattern on the white, which besides is much confused with centuries of breakage and repair, and one is only conscious of it as texture, which indeed is its *raison d'être*. Five feet wide, and towering to a height of more than 50 feet, each "sister" is a shimmering mass of pearl and silver, delicately veined and jewelled with colour to give quality to its whiteness.

The same tendency that caused the artist to "Quarries." substitute mosaic diaper for the scroll work in the setting of his medallions in coloured windows led him in time to fill large spaces of his grisaille windows with painted "quarries." "Quarries" (from the French *carré*) are small diamond-shaped panes, and were then the quickest and most economical way of glazing any given space. Sometimes towards the end of the century the painted pattern ran over the quarries independently of them, but more often in the thirteenth century each quarry was a repetition of the next, the whole thus forming a regular diaper. Sometimes each quarry has a thick black line painted parallel to two, or sometimes all four, of its sides at a distance of three quarters of an inch or so, leaving the space between it and the lead blank while the rest of the quarry is patterned. The effect of this when glazed together is that of interlacing white bands on a ground of pattern.

Apart from economy, the principal motive for the use of grisaille in windows was, as I have said, the need for light. In the Cathedral of Chartres, where there is no grisaille except that in the chapels already mentioned, and where practically all the other windows are filled with richly coloured glass, it is quite difficult to read in the nave on a dull day. It is possible, therefore, that in some churches a certain number of windows may have been deliberately reserved for grisaille.

Combination of grisaille and figure work.

It is not, however, till the very end of the thirteenth century, and then only rarely, that coloured figures and grisaille were combined in the same light as shown in the example from Poitiers in Plate XV., though this is a salient feature of the style of the succeeding period. In the clerestory windows of the choir of St. Pierre at Chartres, which belong to the closing years of the century, the problem has been attacked in an interesting and unique manner, but as the glass in that church really marks the transition to the succeeding period, I shall deal with it later.

Conclusion of the Early Period.

I must now leave the Early Period. If I have devoted a larger space to it than I have to give to either of those succeeding, it is because to me it is the most interesting of all. In all later work artists seem, by comparison, unsatisfied and trying, sometimes with more, sometimes with less, success, to reconcile opposing ideals in their work. Never again does one find the same perfect understanding of the limitations of the material, together with such daring and grandeur of conception, and such depth and earnestness in the ideas expressed.

PLATE XV.   THE FLIGHT INTO EGYPT, POITIERS
Late Thirteenth Century

VIII

THE STYLE OF THE SECOND PERIOD

VIII

THE STYLE OF THE SECOND PERIOD

ALTHOUGH the earliest known work in the style of the Second Period may possibly date from a little before 1300, and although the transition to the succeeding style had certainly begun by 1380, yet, roughly speaking, the limits of the period are those of the fourteenth century, and it is not unusual to speak loosely of the style as the fourteenth century style in glass.

The interest of the period lies perhaps rather in its tendencies and development than in its actual achievements, which by general consent are inferior not only to those of the First, but to those of the Third, Period. It is a period of transition and uncertainty, of the loss of old ideals when men "follow wandering fires."

Most of all does one notice the change of mental attitude. The fierce missionary zeal for

the Faith, the mystic symbolism, has gone. The
wonderful two hundred years which produced St.
Bernard, St. Francis, St. Dominic, St. Louis and
the Crusades, and which saw most of the great
cathedrals built are over, and a reaction sets in.
Never again do we find a whole people, from
princes to ploughmen, neglecting their personal
affairs and combining to build and decorate worthily
a glorious house of God. Churchmen are growing
comfortable and apathetic, if not corrupt, and
laymen are either uninterested in religion or
critical. Towards the end of the century this
feeling gives rise to Wyclif's movement and we
get *Piers Plowman*, with its fierce denunciation
of the means by which money was obtained for
windows and of "lordings" who "writen in
windowes of their well deedes."

With the religious motive thus weakened the
artist seems to have interested himself chiefly in
the technical side of his art,—he may even have
talked of "Art for Art's sake,"—and the usual
result follows. The lack of the underlying and
unifying motive produces a want of proportion in
the parts. The canopies become much more
important than the figures under them; narrative
subjects become much more rare, and when they

occur have none of the dramatic intensity of those of the past age.   Instead we have an endless series of single figures of saints, without character and each in exactly the same affected attitude, like an elongated letter S.   In search of inspiration the artist turns to the study of nature and the literal reproduction of plant forms in ornament.   In the figures too, although the attitudes are conventional the drawing of drapery is less so, and towards the end of the period the artist is tentatively feeling his way towards modelling.

One thing indeed we find during this time, which is within the power of every artist in times of artistic dearth, namely, a steady grappling with practical problems offered by the changed conditions, whereby the way was cleared for the new life that came into the art in the succeeding age.   For instance, by showing how coloured figure work could be combined with grisaille in the same window they solved the problem of lighting ; by the invention of the silver stain they made it possible to make white glass more interesting and to blend it better with colour ; while in drawing they made steady progress towards a style more in keeping with the standards of the time.

The outward and visible characteristics of this

Progress in technique.

period as compared with the preceding one are as follows :—

(1) The simplification of the iron-work.

(2) The invention and use of silver stain.

(3) The combination of figure work and grisaille.

(4) The extraordinary development of the canopy.

(5) The style of drawing the figure.

(6) The use of natural plant forms in ornament.

(7) The quality of the glass, and the colours used.

(8) The use of painted diaper patterns on the coloured backgrounds.

(1) *The Simplification of the Iron-Work.*—The windows of the twelfth century had been huge single lights, but the thirteenth century had seen the gradual evolution of tracery, beginning with the grouping of lancets in pairs under a rose light above. Gradually each lancet was again subdivided into a pair of lights and a rose, the spandrils were pierced, till, at the close of the century, the glazier had to design his window to fit a row of narrow lancets divided by slender mullions, which above Tracery. branched into an elaborate mass of tracery containing a multitude of roses, quatrefoils, trefoils and little

openings of all shapes and sizes.   With this division of the window into comparatively narrow lights the need for the elaborate iron lattice of the preceding age disappeared, its work being now largely taken up by the stone-work.   Instead of lights from six to nine feet wide the glazier had now to deal with lights three and a half feet wide at most, and often much narrower, and in consequence all that was necessary was a series of horizontal bars connecting the mullions, which themselves take the place of the upright bars of former days.   In windows of The this time, then, and later, massive rebated bars are iron-work. fixed horizontally in the stone-work at intervals of between three and four feet, and these with the mullions really form the framework into the square openings of which the panels of the glazing were inserted separately.   Between, and parallel with, these massive bars, three or four light "saddle-bars" are fixed on the inside of the glass, which keep the panel in its place, the glass being attached to them by means of strips of lead (called bands) soldered to the lead-work of the glazing and twisted round the bar.   In order to distinguish between the massive rebated bars which hold the top and bottom of each panel and these light bars between, I shall speak of the former as "frame-bars," the

9

latter by the name they still hold, of "saddle-bars."

The only change from this arrangement which has been made in modern times (except for the use of copper wire instead of lead for the "bands") is the omission of the stout frame-bar, the whole of the weight of the window being now borne by its edges and the saddle-bars. Not only is this arrangement less sound in construction but it is also far less decorative. The thick bars at intervals with thin bars between punctuate the length of the tall windows pleasantly, and are made use of in the design, which in this way is still based on the iron-work. In a recent disastrous "restoration" that was made of one of the windows in the nave of York, the glass was refixed with saddle-bars all of equal size and the thick frames omitted, and it is wonderful how the eye misses them.

This arrangement was, of course, only used in windows above a certain size, in quite small lights the saddle-bars alone being considered sufficient. It was not, I think, an uncommon arrangement for the uppermost bar at all events—that at the springing of the arch—to pass continuously through all the mullions and bind them together.

Silver stain.   (2) *The Invention of Silver Stain.*—In the early years of the fourteenth century an important addition was made to the technical resources of the glass painter by the discovery that if white glass is painted with a preparation of silver—oxide or chloride may be used, or even silver in its metallic form, though that is less convenient—and then subjected to the heat of the kiln, the parts so painted will be found to be stained yellow, pale or dark according to the amount of silver used and according also to the composition of the glass. This is a process quite different from enamelling. It is a true *stain*, actually penetrating the glass to a slight degree and quite indelible except by the perishing of the glass itself.   The oxide or chloride of silver is only mixed with other substances, such as yellow lake, for convenience of application.

Precisely when and where the invention was made and first used we have no means of knowing. We may dismiss the story of the glazier from whose coat a silver button dropped on to the glass he was putting into the kiln, partly because the artist of whom the story is told, one James of Ulm, who worked in Italy and was beatified after his death, was not born till more than a hundred years later. It appears in York Minster, used very sparingly and tentatively, soon after 1300.   I am not sure

Its first appearance.

that there are any examples in France that can be dated quite so early, but it was certainly used there by 1310. Its first use was limited to such matters as differentiating the hair, or gold crowns, of figures from their faces, but the nave windows of York Minster show a progressive increase in its use. Yellow pot-metal is there still used for the larger pieces of yellow in the canopy, but an examination of the details in Plates XVII., XVIII. will show that stain is used in places to gild the crockets of the white pinnacles, the beak and claws of the white eagle in the border of XVII.c, and the flowers in the lower part of the border in XVII.a. The pieces that are yellow all over may, I think, be assumed to be pot-metal. It is not, however, till one gets well on in the century, to 1330 or 1340, that one finds such a free use of the stain in the grisaille as that in the windows at St. Ouen at Rouen, of which the detail is given in Plates XXVI.-XXX.

Combination of figures and grisaille. (3) *The Combination of Figures and Grisaille.*— This is one of the most noticeable developments of the period. As I have said, it is occasionally attempted in the preceding style towards the close of the period, but in the fourteenth century it is the rule. Small windows are sometimes still filled entirely with colour, but nearly every window of any size, especially in the early part of the century, contains a large proportion of grisaille. In the nave of the Church of St. Pierre at Chartres (Plate XXIII.) the same principle is followed as in the earlier work in the choir, namely, the arranging of the figure-work and grisaille so as to form vertical stripes of alternate white and colour. This plan, however, was not persisted in. The numerous vertical lines formed by the mullions in the newer style of architecture required horizontal lines to balance them, and accordingly we find the usual method in fourteenth century windows is for the coloured masses to be ranged in horizontal bands running right across the window through all the lights. Plate XXV. from St. Ouen at Rouen shows a very typical window of the period. Sometimes there was, as here, one row of coloured panels, sometimes two or more as in the nave of York Minster. It will be noticed that in order to blend the white and colour satisfactorily the designer includes a good deal of white among the colour and a good deal of colour among the white. This latter is no longer dispersed through the white in coloured threads, half suspected, but is collected into bosses and borders where its effect is strong enough to support the principal masses. In fact the key-note of the design—namely, the strong contrast of light and dark in flat masses, necessitated by the combination of colour and grisaille—is repeated everywhere in detail throughout the window of which the parts are thus brought into harmony with the whole.

The borders.   This same idea leads to a complete change in the character of the borders.   The running scroll work of the preceding age would no longer be appropriate ; the vertical lines need breaking rather than emphasizing, and the design of the border usually takes the form of alternate blocks of colour and white or yellow.   Plate XXVIII. shows some typical borders from Rouen, borders typical of English as well as French work.   It will be noticed that the coloured pieces are usually left blank while the white and yellow are decorated with patterns or foliage blocked out with solid black.   The ornament of the tracery lights, which by the way are usually kept pretty full of colour, is designed on the same principle.   It consists, in fact, of borders tightly curled up with, sometimes, in the larger lights, a figure or a small coloured medallion in the centre containing a head.

The bosses.   The intervals formed by the regular spacing of the thick iron frame-bars are further emphasized by the placing of a coloured boss or small medallion midway between each. This arrangement in some form or other is almost universal in fourteenth century grisaille, the panels contained between the frame-bars being in fact the units of the design. Some of these bosses from Rouen are shown in Plates XXVI., XXVII., XXIX. Here they are purely fantastic in design, but elsewhere, as at York, they frequently have an heraldic motive or even take the form of shields of arms (Plate XVIII.). Heraldic motives are very commonly used too in the borders, as may be seen in the details from York Minster in Plate XVII., the charges from the shield being repeated all up the border, relieved against, or sometimes alternating with blocks of the colour of the field. Symbolic objects such as chalices are sometimes used in the same way, and occasionally we find borders formed of a succession of little figures under canopies, as in the very elaborate example from York in Plate XVIII.

As the century proceeds quarries become much Quarries. the commonest form of grisaille. In Plates XXV., XXVI. they are true quarries, but in the first quarter of the fourteenth century they are sometimes, as, for instance, at York, "bulged" round the central boss, thus forming a sort of cross between quarries and geometric glazing. Grisaille glazed in geometric patterns such as we find at Merton College, at Evreux, and in St. Pierre at Chartres belongs, I think, always to quite the early years of the period, and even then, as may be seen in Plate XXIII., it shows a decided leaning towards quarry-work, and indeed needs little but the straightening of the leads to convert it into quarries altogether.

Continuous painted patterns are now the rule, as shown in Plate XXVI. The cross-hatched grounds disappear, and presently the silver stain is used (as here) to enrich the painting. It will be noticed that the trellis-like pattern produced by painting lines parallel to the leading is still retained.

The canopy.   (4) *The Extraordinary Development of the Canopy.*—As we have seen, single figures in the preceding period, even at Canterbury, usually had architectural canopies of an unobtrusive kind, of similar design to the sculptured niches which sheltered the statues on the outside of the building. The motive for their adoption by the glazier at this date is not very obvious. They do not in the Early Period form a very important feature in the design, and serve no decorative purpose that

the artist could not equally well have attained by
the flat ornamentation of which he was a master.
However, the glazier seems to have liked the idea
when he saw it in stone-work, where it had a
practical object, and to have imported it into
his own work, where it had none.   It must be
remembered that when the sculpture was painted
in colours, as it was then, the resemblance between
it and the stained glass would have been closer
than it is now.

However this may be, the canopy in the
thirteenth century was a comparatively unobtrusive object, but in the fourteenth century,
as the sculptured canopy grew and developed, so
did its counterpart in stained glass, till the stained-
glass worker seems to have run canopy mad.
Not only is it now found over single figures but
over subjects too.

It is true there was now a certain practical
reason for the tall canopy to be found in the
tall and narrow shape of the lights that had to
be filled.   The human figure was very short and
broad in proportion to them, and when it was a
case of a group the resulting shape was shorter
still, so the canopy offered a convenient way of
elongating the design ; but the fourteenth century

designer developed it, as may be seen in the illustrations, out of all reason, filling it with fantastic detail—angels looking out of the windows, birds perching on the pinnacles, and miniature figures standing like statues in the niches of it—till it quite reduced the figures below it to insignificance. In doing so he was only following the rest of the artistic world, which had all gone wild over the new style of architecture,—with its "passion of pinnacle and fret," as Ruskin called it,—using its details as motives for ornament even where they were least appropriate; but all this expenditure of effort on fantastic and irrelevant detail is really a symptom of the weakening of interest in the principal theme, of which a further sign is the uninteresting treatment of the subjects themselves.

The fourteenth century canopy is, at first at least, always in pure elevation, attempts at perspective not being found till close on the end of the century. Plate XXV. shows both of the forms which are most commonly found, that with a single big crocketted gable and arch spanning the opening, and that with three small ones. I think the former is the earlier form, but they are often, as here, found together.

The base.   In the earlier part of the century at all events, there is never an architectural base to the panel as well as a canopy, but both subject and the shafts of the canopy end off below with a straight line at one of the frame-bars. The earliest examples of anything in the nature of a base that I know of are at Wells and in the great east window of Gloucester Cathedral, where the topmost pinnacle of each canopy spreads out into a sort of bracket supporting the next figure above, while the shafts at the side are prolonged upwards into the canopy of that figure, an arrangement suggestive of Perpendicular work. But indeed in its general arrangement, though not in its details, the Gloucester east window, though executed in 1350–1360, contains many hints of the style that was to follow, the stone tracery, in fact, being pure Perpendicular, perhaps the earliest example known.

The canopy work itself is always in the main yellow or white, relieved against a coloured background, and with windows, capitals and other details put in with another colour. In the aisle windows of the nave of York Cathedral, the coloured background, and, at first, the pinnacles of the canopy too, end off square at the top, at one of the frame-bars, just as the panel does at the bottom. As the series proceeds, however, the central pinnacles, as in the "Peter de Dene" window, of which details are given in Plate XVIII., are prolonged above the bar, a tendency which became more and more developed as time went on. In the big window from St. Ouen's at Rouen, shown in Plate XXV., the coloured background, by a rather inept arrangement, is also brought up behind the pinnacles, and has to end in a somewhat meaningless outline.

At first the yellow of the canopies was obtained by the use of a yellow glass, a "pot-metal" (*i.e.* a glass coloured all through in the making) of a not very pleasant colour, but gradually this was superseded by the use of silver stain, by means of which a much lighter and more delicate effect could be obtained. Its introduction was gradual, however, the artist having to feel his way towards the best use of it. As its use increased, coloured glass was less and less used for details of the canopy, the character of which gradually approached more and more to that which it was to have in the following period.

In some of the very earliest windows of the period, such as those in Merton College Chapel and in the chapels of the choir in Evreux Cathedral, small coloured panels, with canopies of quite modest and reasonable proportions, are used to decorate large spaces of grisaille. The growth of the canopy began very soon, however, and where these small canopies are found together with geometric glazing of the grisaille and a complete absence of silver stain, it is fairly safe to assign a date to the window not much later than 1305.

Curiously enough, in spite of the fourteenth century fondness for elaborate canopies, we find at the same time another type of window in which they are wholly absent, the figures being placed simply upon a background of quarries. Plate XXIV., one of a series from the clerestory of St. Ouen at Rouen, is an example of this. Here the figures stand, it is true, on little architectural bases (an exception to the rule I mentioned just now), but elsewhere these too are absent. *Figures on quarries.*

(5) *The Style of Drawing the Figure.*—The chief characteristic of this in fourteenth century work is its apparent affectation. There seems to have been a sudden revolt from the taste for dramatic force of action which characterized the subject panels of the thirteenth century. Look at Plate XXXI. from Rouen, with its three little panels showing the Annunciation and the Visitation. In each the figure is in exactly *The S-like pose.*

the same pose, and that a perfectly meaningless one, like an elongated letter S. Yet this pose seems to have become all the fashion, for it is almost universal in the work of this period, and is found even in such transitional work as the east windows of the antechapel of New College, Oxford, which, in other respects, belong far more to the succeeding period.

Yet in spite of this loss of naturalism in movement, in the actual drawing of forms, both of the figure and of drapery, there is an advance. If you will compare St. Luke from the clerestory of St. Ouen at Rouen in Plate XXIV. with Methuselah from Canterbury in Plate III., you will see the change that has occurred. St. Luke has far less character and force, he is far less alive, his pose and gesture mean nothing, or at most are mildly argumentative, and yet there is a certain sense in which he, and still more his drapery, is better drawn, or if not better, at all events in a more advanced manner. This is more noticeable if you compare St. Luke or the little figures in Plate XXX. with the big angel from Chartres in Plate X.. which is not so well drawn as the Methuselah.

The fact is that the twelfth and thirteenth

century convention in figure drawing had served
its turn well, but was now worn out.   Deriving,
originally, as we have seen, out of Greek art
in its Byzantine form, it had formed a stock on
which the artist of the Early Period had been
able to graft his own observation and love of
nature, but it had now ceased to satisfy and was
therefore abandoned.   The progress of drawing
in other arts, or at all events in sculpture, had
taught men to demand something different.   The
artist of the late thirteenth century, as the last
influence of Greek art died out of his work,
had undoubtedly neglected grace of form in his
enthusiasm for vigorous and naturalistic movement ; and, as so often happens when one quality
in art is neglected, a reaction had come, in which
people demanded that quality above all others.
Consequently, the chief effort of the draughtsman of the fourteenth century, if I understand
him rightly, was to bring his drawing of form
up to the standard required of him, the S-like
attitude, for instance, being merely a trick to get
a willowy gracefulness into his figures, especially
those of women.

The same tendency is observable in the drawing
of drapery.   The drapery of the thirteenth century

The effort
towards
grace of
form.

was entirely conventional in the method in which it was drawn, but it was always in movement and helped the action of the figures. Fourteenth century drapery, on the other hand, is always at rest, or at most sweeping with the slow movement of a figure, but its folds are drawn in a much more advanced manner than before, and seem to bear evidence of a certain amount of direct study of actual drapery, either on the part of the artist or of those whom he was following. The ideal of gracefulness shows itself in a love for long and sweeping folds, as may be seen in Plates XXIV., XXX., XXXI.

At first the artist is content to use in his drawing the strong line work of the preceding period, but as the century proceeds this becomes rather more delicate, and he begins to feel his way towards modelling in half-tones. The drapery over the Virgin's knees in Plate XXI. shows this very clearly.

Neglect of movement. With this preoccupation with the truer rendering of form, it is perhaps not surprising that the study of action was neglected. The artist had enough to do to draw his figures and drapery in repose without making them move about and do things, and a contributory cause was, no doubt, the weakening of interest already alluded to in the subjects he had to illustrate. This then is why, whereas in the thirteenth century we find a highly conventional rendering of form allied to naturalism in movement, in the fourteenth, conversely, we find conventional poses and movement allied to a more naturalistic rendering of form.

Comparative study of the illuminated manuscripts of the same period shows exactly the same changes in progress. So closely do the two arts keep pace with each other that I do not think it can be said that at any time either was leading the other. They must have been in very close touch even if they were not, which it is quite possible they often were, practised by the same artists. The lead, if there was a lead, must have come from sculpture.

(6) *The use of Natural Plant Forms in Ornament.* —This is another manifestation of the same spirit, and divides the work of the fourteenth century most sharply from that both of the preceding and following periods. The Jesse Trees, and the leafy scrolls and borders of the twelfth and thirteenth centuries belong to no genus known to botanists, but in the fourteenth century it seems as if the

Natural plant forms in ornament.

10

artist, the inspiration of religion failing him, had sought it in a rather literal study of Nature. Accordingly in the grisaille and borders of this period we find patterns formed of oak leaves and acorns, ivy leaves, maple, vine, and so on. Plate XXVI. is rather an exception in that one cannot name the particular plant; but Plates XXVIII. and XXIX. contain characteristic examples, and Plate XXI. shows a good vine border from York, and some holly leaf grisaille.

Yet the feeling for Nature in these patterns does not go very deep. The artist is, for instance, content to make the oak wreath and twine itself as freely as the vine, and I always feel that his practice is the result of theory rather than the spontaneous expression of love of Nature. The earlier worker was really, I believe, more in tune with Nature than his successor of the fourteenth century. He did not copy her forms in ornament but he followed her principles. He did not copy her forms, because she had taught him to design forms for himself. Nature, it may be observed, does not adorn one object with copies of another, hardly even when she gives her creatures protective colouring and markings, but gives to each the patterning which suits it best. In the same way the ornament of the twelfth and thirteenth century artist is always perfectly suited to its purpose without distracting one's attention; and when his subject requires him to represent a tree or a bush,— such as the fig tree under which Nathanael sits, or the thicket in which the ram is caught, at Canterbury,—though the foliage is that of the shamrock, he knows how to make it grow and live better than his fourteenth century successor. The waves, too, of the Flood in Plate IV., conventional though they are, give a real sense of tossing and stormy water.

(7) *The Quality of Glass and the Colours Used.*— At first these differ little from those used in the previous period, but as the fourteenth century proceeds, the rich intense reds and blues, with their "streakiness," their endless variety of tone and texture, which makes each piece of glass a jewel with an individuality of its own, and needing no enrichment, give way to glass of a thinner, flatter quality. In Plate III. Mr. Saint has managed to catch and the printer to reproduce something of the quality of these early blues. There is a change too in the proportions of the colours used. The colour schemes of the Early Period are almost always conceived on a basis of red and blue, but

Change in material.

Fourteenth century colour schemes.

now green and yellow become equally important; Plates XXI., XXII., for example, contain very little blue at all. The canopies when not white are mainly yellow, and this alone is responsible for a very large amount of yellow in the colour scheme —too much, in fact, as a rule. The yellow used at first, till silver stain took its place, was, as I have said, a rather hot unpleasant pot-metal. The green of the First Period had been a rather sharp brilliant colour, used generally in small quantities, and striking a high shrill note among the deep reds and blues, like a clarionet in an orchestra. The typical green of the fourteenth century, on the other hand, which is often used as a background, is a greyer duller colour altogether. Plate XVI. and Plate XXI. give a fairly good idea of its quality.

White glass for flesh.   Another change, which was the natural result, both of the increased amount of white now used in windows and of the introduction of the silver stain, was the gradual substitution of white glass in the flesh of figures for the brownish pink formerly used. Its use afforded an opportunity for getting white in amongst the colour, and so helping to bind the design together, and the fact that the hair, crowns, and mitres of figures could now be stained yellow, rendered it on the whole the most suitable glass for the purpose, and we find it holding the field down to the late sixteenth century, when a pinkish enamel began to be used.

(8) *The use of Painted Diaper Patterns on the Coloured Backgrounds.*—The red and blue back- Painted diapers. grounds to the figures in the twelfth and thirteenth centuries needed no further decoration.   Their own depth and quality was enough in itself, but the thinner, flatter tones that succeeded them needed enriching and giving texture to, in order to throw the figures up into proper relief; or so the fourteenth century artist seems to have felt, for from the beginning we find his backgrounds usually covered with a diaper painted in enamel.

The method is always the same; the ground having been covered with an even coat of enamel, the pattern is scratched out clear with the point of a stick or a brush handle.   Plates XVI., XX., XXI. are typical examples, and show in detail the kind of pattern that was used.

It is very rarely that we find anything of the kind in the previous period.   There is, as we have seen, an isolated and early example of it at Canterbury, where a rather paler, poorer blue has been used than in the other windows, but there it is more delicate than in the fourteenth century, the pattern being scratched out of a very thin semi-transparent mat of enamel; and it is found too in some late thirteenth century windows in St. Urbain at Troyes, but in fourteenth century work it is frequently met with even at the beginning of the period, and by the end of the first quarter of the century it is the rule, and remains so throughout the succeeding century as well.

IX

EARLY FOURTEENTH CENTURY GLASS IN ENGLAND

(MERTON COLLEGE AND EXETER)

IX

EARLY FOURTEENTH CENTURY GLASS IN ENGLAND

(MERTON COLLEGE AND EXETER)

THE windows in the chapel of Merton College, Oxford, are perhaps the earliest in which the design of the Second Period has taken a definite and typical form. Antony à Wood, in his catalogue of Fellows, says that the donor, Henry de Mamesfield or Mannesfield, whose portrait is in the windows, caused them to be made in 1283, but in view of an order in the Bursar's Rolls of 1292 for stone for building these windows, this date must be rejected. Antony à Wood's statement elsewhere that the *whole* chapel was pulled down and rebuilt in 1424 shows he is not altogether to be relied on. The presence of the fleur-de-lis with the castle of Castile in some of the borders

153

makes it probable[1] that they were done after Edward I.'s second marriage with Margaret of France in 1299, while the arms of an Heir-Apparent as well as of a King of England in the east window makes it certain that they were executed while Edward I. and his son were both alive, *i.e.* before 1307. On the whole, and by comparison with the York glass, I should think 1303–1305 a not improbable date for them.

The east window. There are seven windows on each side and a great east window, and, with the exception of the latter, they are still fairly perfect. Of the east window it is only the beautiful "wheel" tracery which retains its original glass, the lower lights, alas! having been destroyed in 1702 to make room for a monstrosity by one Pryce—a horrible blare of yellow. What remains in the tracery has a more transitional character than the other windows, and was probably executed first, and if only the lower lights had remained they might have thrown an interesting light on the development of the style.

The three trefoils in the centre of the wheel

[1] This is not altogether conclusive. The fleur-de-lis and castle had been a favourite ornament in French glass since their adoption by St. Louis.

contain three coats of arms—the short triangular shields of the thirteenth century, of which the first is that of Edward I., the leopards of England ; the second the same with a label of five points azure for his son, afterwards Edward II.; and the third that of Walter de Merton, the founder of the college. For the most part the other lights contain ornament that is wholly fourteenth century in character, but the quatrefoil on each side has a feature which shows the early date of the window. In these two small figures representing the Annunciation, though themselves in the style and colouring of the early fourteenth century, are placed directly on a background of red and blue mosaic diaper, such as one finds again and again in thirteenth century work in France, and among the fragments in the South Rose at Lincoln. I have often thought that thirteenth century glaziers sometimes kept this mosaic filling-in stock, and perhaps the artist of Merton had some left on his hands and used it up here. In any case it would seem to show that the style in which he was working was fairly new to his workshop.

The fourteen side windows are designed on a plan which is typical of fourteenth century work both in England and in France, especially Normandy.

The side windows.

The sections into which the glazing is divided by the heavy iron frame-bars are taken as the units of the design. One in each light is filled with a coloured panel—a figure under a canopy—and the rest with grisaille having a coloured boss in the centre of each, the whole being surrounded by a coloured border. The effect is that of a range of greenish-white windows just dotted and edged with colour, and with a single broad band of colour running horizontally through them all. This plan is common in all early fourteenth century work, especially in England and Normandy. Evreux is another example, York nave another, but with two rows of coloured panels, and the window from Rouen in Plate XXV. is only an elaboration of it forty years later. At Merton College, however, the canopy has not yet run mad, but is of modest proportions, figure and canopy together only occupying one section of glazing.

The grisaille itself is for the most part of "bulged" quarries curving round the central bosses, but two on each side have true quarries. All have the trellis pattern formed by doubling the lead with a painted line and a continuous flowing pattern of foliage—vine, oak, ivy, and fig—spreading through it over the window from a central stem.

Plate XXVI. is a later example of the same thing, but with the addition of silver stain, which is nowhere found in the Merton windows.

The borders, when not formed of castle and fleur-de-lis, are of a kind found in the Chapter-House at York, and common in other fourteenth century windows—leaves white or yellow, branching at intervals from a straight or wavy stem on a coloured ground. There is not much variety in the coloured bosses, which all consist either of a simple four-leaved pattern or of a small head in white on a coloured disc. There are, I think, only four different designs of these heads—Christ, an old man, a king, and a queen continually repeated.

The most woeful poverty of ideas is, however, found in the figures under the canopies. There are fourteen windows of three lights each, with a figure in each,—forty-two in all,—yet the designer could think of nothing better to do than to put an apostle in the centre light of each window, repeating two apostles to make them go round, and in every window but two a kneeling figure of the donor— "Magister Enricus de Mamesfield"—in the light on each side. Thus the proud and happy Master Henry might see himself reproduced no less than four-and-twenty times, in robes of red, white,

Poverty of ideas.

brown or blue, wide sleeved robes with a hood, doubtless the M.A.'s gown of the period.

Neither are the apostles very interestingly treated. They are almost repetitions of each other, standing in the same conventional pose and distinguished only by their attributes. The backgrounds of the figures are diapered with enamel in the usual fourteenth century way.

In point of development these windows come between the Chapter-House and the earliest nave windows at York, and correspond with the earliest work at Evreux, being the earliest windows in which the style of the Second Period has taken final and definite form. They are not without their beauty, but in looking at them one wonders what has become of the spirit that created the windows of Canterbury, Chartres, and Bourges.

Exeter east window.   Of the same stage of development as the Merton windows are the earliest of the figures remaining in the east window of Exeter Cathedral. Although this window was rebuilt and enlarged in 1390, the original glass was, it is known, used again and eked out with new. There is an entry in the Fabric Rolls of 1301–1302 for 1271 feet of glass at $5\frac{1}{2}$d. per foot, "ad summas fenestras frontis novi operis"— which seems to mean the east end of the choir, and two years later a payment to Master Walter the glazier for fixing the glass "summi gabuli," but no further light is thrown on its origin. Later on, however, in the roll for 1317–1318, there is an entry for glass, apparently for the Lady Chapel, "bought at Rouen" at the rate of 6d. a foot for white (? grisaille) and 1s. 0d. for coloured, and from this it has been argued that the whole of the glass up to that time was bought from Rouen too. To me, however, the fact that Rouen is specifically mentioned here, and nowhere else, militates against this theory, while if the price of 5½d. a foot paid for the glass of the east window was for finished figure work, it is far lower than that of the Rouen glass. The figures themselves are much larger than those at Merton College, and on the whole more interestingly treated. There are nine of them remaining: three patriarchs; three apostles—St. Peter, St. Paul, and St. Andrew; and three female saints —St. Margaret, St. Catherine, and, I think, the Magdalen. The canopies are large in proportion, being nearly twice the height of the figures,—an unusual height for so early a date,—but they are not unlike the Merton canopies in style. There is no trace of silver stain either in the canopies or the figures.

Another fact which to some extent tells against the theory of their Rouen origin, is that so far I have found no glass of that date at Rouen which at all resembles them, whereas as late as 1290–1295 Clement of Chartres was, as we have seen, doing work there, which shows little change from the style of the middle of the thirteenth century.

Grisaille at Exeter.

There is some very interesting grisaille in two of the chapels at Exeter, of an earlier type than that at Merton, being in fact transitional between the style of the First and Second Periods. It has the interlacing medallions of coloured strap work, with the painted grisaille pattern passing behind them, but this latter, though chiefly of the " Herba Benedicta," breaks here and there into natural leafage. It is a slightly earlier point of development than even the Chapter-House at York, and corresponds very closely with some at St. Urbain at Troyes.

PLATE XVI. HERALDIC PANEL, FROM THE CLERESTORY OF THE NAVE, YORK MINSTER
Early Fourteenth Century

X

FOURTEENTH CENTURY GLASS
AT YORK

X

FOURTEENTH CENTURY GLASS
AT YORK

THE best work of the Second Period that I know
of anywhere is to be found in York Minster.
Here the new style seems to have become engrafted
on a strong local school which had preserved much
of the life and vigour of the previous age. It is
true that even here one finds a certain weakening
of the religious motive, but its place seems to be
to some extent taken by a patriotic enthusiasm for
a warrior king and for the gallant nobles who
followed him in the Scotch wars, and whose arms
are everywhere in the glass of the nave.

The windows themselves show a steady and
almost unbroken progression in style from the late
thirteenth to the early part of the fifteenth century,
which makes them most useful for study. Leaving
out the fragments of very early glass I have

163

mentioned before, the order of their execution seems to be—

1. The " Five Sisters."
2. The Chapter-House.
3. The vestibule of the Chapter-House.
4. The clerestory of the nave.
5. The first five [1] in the north aisle of the nave (dated by Winston 1306).
6. The first five [1] in the south aisle of the nave.
7. The sixth in the north aisle of the nave.
8. { The three west windows of the nave (contract 1338).
The sixth in the south aisle of the nave.
One (probably from the nave) in the south aisle of the choir.
9. The third from the east in the south side of the Lady Chapel.
10. The fifteenth century windows in the choir and Lady Chapel, which we shall come to later.

Whatever difference of opinion there may be about the date of these windows, I do not think this order can be disputed.

The " Five Sisters " have already been dealt with in their place in the First Period. Those of the Chapter-House, whether of earlier or later date than those of the Merton College Chapel, are distinctly earlier in style and are one of the few examples of work that is really transitional between

[1] From the east.

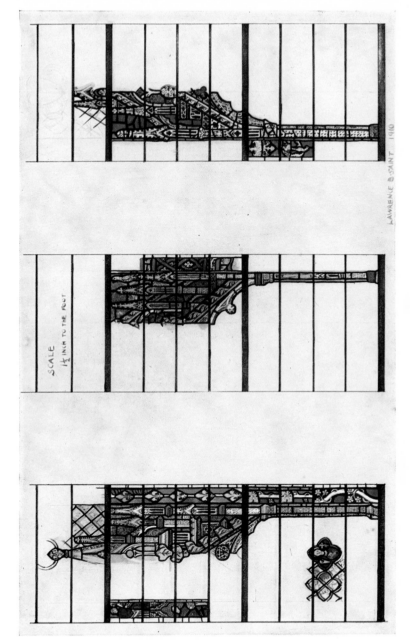

SCALE

1½ INCH TO THE FOOT

LAWRENCE B. SAINT 1910

PLATE XVII. DETAILS FROM WINDOWS IN THE NORTH AISLE OF NAVE, YORK MINSTER

Fourteenth Century

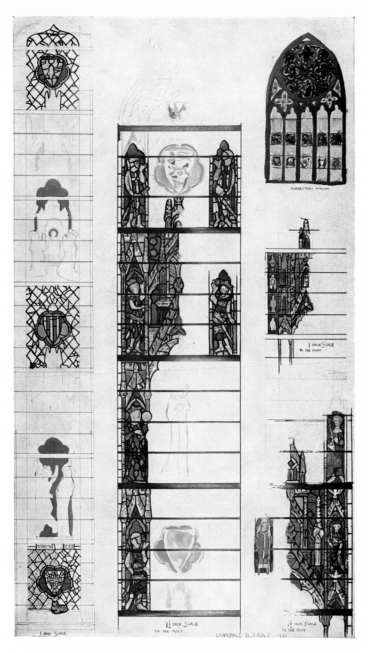

PLATE XVIII.   BORDER AND SHIELDS, FROM PETER DE DENE WINDOW, NORTH
AISLE OF NAVE, YORK MINSTER, WITH DETAILS FROM WINDOW IN SOUTH
AISLE AND SKETCH OF CLERESTORY WINDOW

Fourteenth Century

the First and Second Periods, belonging almost as much to one as to the other.   Unfortunately there is no record of the building of the Chapter-House, and its date is a matter of dispute, Drake putting it as early as the time of Archbishop Walter Grey, who died in 1256, and Browne holding it was not finished till nearly 1340—an impossible date for the glass.   As in Merton Chapel the presence of the fleur-de-lis as well as the castle of Castile in the windows may mean that they are not earlier than 1299, but I do not think they are much later.   The only French work I know of which at all corresponds to it is in St. Urbain at Troyes, which Viollet-le-Duc dates at about 1295, and the windows from Poitiers in Plate XV.

The windows are divided by the tracery into narrow lights in which a series of coloured medallions of typical thirteenth century shape are placed one above the other on a ground of grisaille, much as in the window from Poitiers.   It is in the grisaille itself that the beginnings of the new style are shown, for whereas in the " Five Sisters," which are certainly later than 1260, the pattern on the grisaille is the conventional trefoil of the First Period—the Herba Benedicta—and conforms to the shapes of the lead-work and of the hollow medal-

The grisaille in the Chapter-House.

lions outlined in coloured bands, in the Chapter-House, although the medallions in coloured outline are still there, the painted pattern, as at Exeter and Troyes, runs through them independently of them (giving them a rather meaningless appearance of being hung in front of it), but is wholly formed of natural foliage, oak, fig, ivy, and so on; the borders, too, are of the character of the Second Period. Similar grisaille is found at Chartham in Kent. At Poitiers, as may be seen in the illustration, the grisaille pattern is still of the Herba Benedicta, with a cross-hatched ground, and the border is of an earlier type; at St. Urbain at Troyes, as at Exeter, both the conventional and the natural foliage are found, but on the whole I am somewhat inclined to think that wherever the other features of the style originated these patterns of natural foliage were first used in England.

These windows, by the way, are in a sad state and want releading, instead of which the authorities have contented themselves with placing quarry glazing on the outside of them, which now that it is dirty so darkens the old windows as to kill all light and colour in them. When I say releading, I mean that and nothing more—*not* "restoration," which is murder.

The windows in the L-shaped vestibule, or The Chapter-House vestibule. passage, which leads to the Chapter-House show a slight further development. Here the grisaille is of the same character as in the Chapter-House itself, but the coloured panels are each surmounted by a little crocketted canopy, which here appears for the first time in York. It is found in some glass at Selling, in Kent (which from the heraldry seems to commemorate Edward I.'s marriage to Margaret of France in 1299), in conjunction with grisaille in which the foliage is of the earlier conventional type, and which therefore may, perhaps, be a little earlier than these windows.

The windows in the clerestory of the nave of The clerestory of the nave. York Minster are little, I think, if at all, later than those in the Chapter-House, but it is a little difficult to compare them as they are designed to be seen at such a very different distance from the eye, the white parts of the clerestory windows consisting only of interlacing bands of lead-work without any painted pattern at all. A small inset in Plate XVIII. shows the general arrangement of all these windows; the great wheel of the tracery, it will be seen, is filled with colour, while the lower lights are white with two bands of coloured panels running horizontally through them

all.   Of these panels the lower row consists of coats
of arms of the great families of the North, contained in medallions of which Plate XVI. is an
example. The upper row consists for the most
part of subjects contained in somewhat similar
medallions, but many of the panels are filled with
earlier glass of the twelfth and thirteenth centuries,
which were doubtless preserved from the older
nave.   Thus, if you let your eye run along the
northern side it will be arrested at the extreme
west end of the line by a piece of blue that is
different from all the others.   It is the twelfth
century blue that we have seen at St. Denis and
in the west windows at Chartres, and the panel is
the portion of a Jesse Tree of the same pattern as
that which is found at both those places, and which
I mentioned when speaking of them.   Portions of
the foliage of the tree are in the tracery above.   I
think I recognize this blue too in a panel on the
south side representing a man with a horse and cart,
and remains of early thirteenth century glass are
plentiful.

The aisles of
the nave.

Next after the clerestory, the oldest windows in
the nave are the first five from the east in each
aisle. In these the style of the Second Period is
fully developed and is in no sense transitional.

They are rather more advanced in style than the Merton College windows and are by a far finer artist, being, in fact, the finest work of the period that I know. They seem to me all to have been executed within a few years of each other, probably in continuous succession, and to show the gradual development which might be expected during the progress of the work.

Those on the north are the oldest and in the best condition, those on the south being much broken and confused, and one, alas! "restored." The general design is the same in all and is a typical fourteenth century one, two horizontal bands of coloured panels surmounted by canopies running horizontally through all the lights, separated by panels of grisaille which have a coloured spot in the centre of each panel. It is characteristic of the fourteenth century that the whole of the lower panels are in nearly every window devoted to the donor, who is thus given as much space as the subject. The grisaille is of the same type as at Merton. As in all early fourteenth century work, the sections divided by the heavy frame-bars are taken as the units of the design, the coloured panels with their canopies each occupying two sections and the grisaille panels one each.

Nos. 2, 3, and 4 on the north were probably the first executed, as they contain no trace of yellow stain (Plate XVII.b). No. 5, from which the border of monks in their stalls in Plate XVII.a is taken, has a single touch of it in one place, but in No. 1 it is used, though still sparingly and tentatively, on the beaks and claws of the eagles in the borders of the outer lights (Plate XVII.c) and on the mail of the knights in the border of the centre light (Plate XVIII.), and here and there in the canopy. Another fresh development is the prolonging of the pinnacles of the canopy into the grisaille panel above.

The Peter de Dene window.

This window, which is sometimes called the Heraldic Window, from the number of coats of arms it contains, is the only one of them that has hitherto been the subject of any very close study, Mr. Winston having devoted a whole article to an extremely close and careful analysis of its heraldry, and to an account of the life of its donor, one Peter de Dene, whose portrait is in the central light and who was a churchman-politician under the first two Edwards. There is no space here to repeat his arguments, and I will only say that, after reading them and rereading them, I find it very difficult not to accept his conclusion that the most probable date for the window is 1306.   The subject panels represent the story of St. Catherine, but are the least interesting part of the window, of which the most charming feature is, perhaps, the border of the central light, which consists of miniature portraits of kings, queens, and nobles whom the donor wished to compliment (Plate XVIII.).   The two upper-most figures are those of a Templar and a Hospitaller ; below them are the kings and queens of England and France, in allusion to Edward I.'s second marriage, and the recent peace concluded by it ; below the Queen of France is the Heir-Apparent of England, and the remaining figures bear the arms of de Clare, Earl of Gloucester, Warrenne (both connected with the Royal Family), Beauchamp, Ros, Mowbray, Clifford, and Percy. The coats of arms which form the bosses in the white panels are those of foreign monarchs with whom the King of England was connected.   The white eagles in the outer border are thought by Winston to refer to Piers Gaveston, who, though somewhat under a cloud in 1306, yet, as the friend of the heir to the throne, was a good person to keep in favour with.   It is true the Gaveston eagles were golden, but heraldry was more free and easy then than later.   There is a portrait of Prince

Edward in the Chapter-House with a white falcon
on his wrist, and white falcons are plentiful in the
windows of the nave, yet I have never heard of his
using it as a badge, though the last Plantagenet,
Richard II., did so.

The Bell-
founder's
window.

The next window to this is the famous "Bell-
founder's Window," given by Richard Tunnoc,
bell-founder of York. In the lower panel of the
centre light is his portrait kneeling and presenting
a model of the window to an Archbishop, perhaps
St. William. The panels on either side represent
one, the casting, the other the turning of a bell in a
lathe. Bells are everywhere in the window, the
canopies are hung with them in rows, the borders
are formed of them, but Mr. Westlake's careless
remark that all six panels represent the process of
bell-making is not true. The upper three are
much perished, but one can just see that they tell
the story of St. William's return to York, when
the welcoming crowds broke down Ouse Bridge,
but when, through his intercession, not a life was
lost.

The de la
Warde
window.

The third window contains some interesting
portraits in its lower panels. The central one is
that of an Archbishop of York, as shown by the
key in his left hand, holding in his right a model

PLATE XIX.
ST. MARGARET,
WEST WINDOW OF
NAVE, YORK
MINSTER
Fourteenth Century

PLATE XX.

ST. STEPHEN,
FROM SOUTH AISLE
OF NAVE,
YORK MINSTER
Fourteenth Century

of the nave.[1] On the left is a knight dismounted, holding his horse by the bridle, and behind him the hand of some one out of the picture holds his banner, which the painting, though almost obliterated, still shows to be " vairé " argent and sable. In the opposite panel is a lady standing and behind her, half out of the picture, a man on horseback, doubtless his wife and son. Now the arms on the banner are those of the Barons de la Warde, of whom there were only two, Robert and his son Simon. Robert, who was in the Scotch wars, and in 1306 was steward of the household to Edward I., must have passed the greater part of that year in York with the King, who was there preparing for his last expedition against Robert Bruce. He, Robert de la Warde, died next year. His son Simon was Governor of York in 1321, and helped with his forces to defeat Thomas of Lancaster at Borough-bridge. It will thus be seen that the window might either have been given by the father in 1306 or the son about 1320, but since two figures are represented, and since we know that Simon died childless (the barony becoming extinct), it seems probable that it was executed in the father's lifetime. Again,

---

[1] In 1306 this would be William de Greenfield, under whom the nave was building, and in 1320 William de Melton, who finished it.

though 1320 would fit the Bellfounder's window, since Tunnoc was Sheriff of York that year, it cannot be made to fit the facts in Peter de Dene's window, which is certainly not earlier but later. The presence of the Templar is against it, as it is unthinkable that the Order which was suppressed in 1312 (and its grandmaster burnt) should thus have been complimented in 1320. But for this fact I am bound to say I should have thought 1320 the more probable.

If then we accept 1306 as the approximate date for these windows, it will be seen that in little more than seven years a complete change had come over the design of English stained glass, and it will presently be seen that much the same thing was happening in France at the same time. Indeed, one of the surprising things about mediæval art is the rapidity with which new ideas seem to flash across Europe from Yorkshire to Dalmatia.

The outer lights of the de la Warde window have a fascinating border of monkeys bearing pitchers, and across the bottom of the window is a busy scene of monkeys hunting and feasting, with a man and woman among them.

The three lower panels of the fifth window illustrate a story which I have never yet found any

one to give me a clue to.   It has nothing to do The fifth window in the north aisle.
with the upper subjects, two of which are the
martyrdoms of SS. Peter and Paul, the third being
merely fragments.   From its position, and from the
fact that the costume is contemporary with the
painting, I should rather imagine that it refers to
some local story, perhaps connected in some way
with the gift of the window.   On the right, a figure
in a red cope with a red skull-cap but no nimbus,
holding a scourge or "disciplina" in his hand, is
pointing apparently in denunciation at what appears
to be a cringing figure in brown, much broken,
among a crowd of others, some of whom are women.
In the next panel, which is also much broken and
jumbled, the same figures seem to be there, but the
one in red seems to be exhorting rather than
denouncing.   The third or left-hand panel is in
much better condition, and here we see the figures
plainly.   The one in brown, which turns out to be
that of a layman, without armour, but with a
dagger at his side and a spiked mace slung over his
left arm, is kneeling at the feet of the figure in red,
who is seated, and with one hand laid on the
penitent's head is with the other firmly administer-
ing the "disciplina" to his back !   The border is of
monks (or canons) in their stalls, and the only

heraldry in the window is contained in the painted diaper on the blue background, and consists of spread eagles and rampant lions, like the border of the Peter de Dene window. The remains of the donor's name—w . . . MN . . . CTON—gives me no clue.

The south aisle.

The first five windows in the south aisle seem to me to follow these immediately in order of execution. The style is just a little more advanced; stain is used more freely, and the canopies begin to grow up into the white panel above them until their pinnacles reach its centre and do away with the coloured boss there altogether; they spread into the borders in many cases in order to give more room to the figures under them, thus giving rise to the three-gabled form of canopy. In colour they are still very beautiful, but have suffered much more damage than those in the north aisle. Several of them have been repaired and restored by Peckitt, of York, as the inscriptions show, at the end of the eighteenth century, but Peckitt's restoration was merciful compared to that which the fourth one has undergone at the hands of

The de Mauley window.

a modern firm of stained-glass manufacturers. Whole quantities of the old glass have been replaced by new, and the whole has been smeared

PLATE XXI.

THE NATIVITY,
UPPER PART OF
EAST WINDOW
OF NORTH AISLE,
ALL SAINTS',
NORTH STREET,
YORK
Fourteenth Century

with some brownish mess to make it look old again.   As a result, all life and beauty have gone out of the window which is merely a sort of embalmed corpse, and this is the more to be regretted that it seems to have been a particularly interesting window.   The lower panels each contain a pair of kneeling figures, five knights, and one churchman who hold aloft shields which show them to be various members of the Yorkshire family of de Mauley of Mulgrave.   The founder of the family was the Poitevin ruffian, Piers de Mauley who, at King John's orders, murdered Prince Arthur and was rewarded for this service with the hand and estates of an unfortunate Yorkshire heiress.   The descendants of this miscreant seem, however, to have been gallant soldiers who distinguished themselves in Scotland and Gascony and were made barons by Edward I.   A peculiarity of the family was that the eldest son was always called Peter, and they distinguished themselves by numbers, like kings.   One of the portraits must be the particular Peter who afterwards, in 1346, commanded the forces which Queen Philippa raised in her husband's absence against the invading Scots, whom he routed at Neville's Cross, taking their king, David Bruce, prisoner,

12

and partly avenging Bannockburn. An interesting point of heraldry is the way in which the arms of the different sons are distinguished, not by the marks of cadency used later, but by the addition of different charges to the original shield which is or, a bend sable.

The fifth window was once a Tree of Jesse but is now a mere wreck. It is, however, the earliest Jesse Tree I know of in which the stem and foliage of the tree are green.

These windows show a progressive increase in the use of white for flesh colour instead of the brownish pink formerly used. At first, white is used only for women's faces, and then for those of saints of both sexes, brown-pink continuing to be used for other people till quite the middle of the century or later. Stain is not used on the hair at first, but sometimes a thin brown matt of enamel is laid all over the hair which at a distance has almost the effect of stain.

The sixth window in the north aisle.

The sixth window on the north side is, I think, a good many years later in date than these ten windows we have been considering, and is much less beautiful. A canopy and border from it are shown in Plate XVIII.a on the right. Although the same general arrangement is adhered to as in the other windows, the treatment is much coarser; the crockets of the canopies are big, heavy, and ugly, of a brownish-yellow pot-metal, but at the same time stain is freely, indeed lavishly, used, not only in the canopies and borders but, for the first time in the Cathedral, in the quarries of the grisaille as well.   The borders of heraldry or little figures have given way to running patterns of natural foliage of the more common fourteenth century type.   There are four different patterns of these borders in the window, so that some probably came from another window of the same date, perhaps in the now empty seventh window.

Later still are the three west windows and the sixth in the south aisle which mark a further stage in development.   Here we have at last a definite date to help us, for the contract with the glazier, one Robert, is still in existence and is dated 1338, so we may assume the windows were finished about 1340.   It is difficult to judge these windows fairly, for they were subjected to a most drastic restoration in the eighteenth century, and the great central one is further disfigured by protective quarry glazing on the outside, which reduces it to a dirty brown.   I do not think, however, that they can ever have been, comparatively speaking, very

The west windows.

good, and I am inclined to look upon them as perhaps the poorest work of the Middle Ages. Plate XIX. shows one light of the northernmost of the three, that at the west end of the north aisle. It will be seen that the canopy has now grown to an absurd height and fills the whole light, and neither in its proportions nor in its details is it very graceful. The border is now growing narrower and narrower, and is eventually doomed to disappear altogether. The crockets of the gable are the only yellow pot-metal used, silver stain being used everywhere else, and not very artistically, though how far this is due to the restorer it is difficult to say.

The same qualities may be observed in the great central west window of the nave, also the work of the glazier Robert. Here, too, the canopies over the various rows of figures which form the design meet the feet of the row above, and in the top row shoot up to the head of the light. Their stiff awkwardness is in curious contrast to the wonderful flowing grace of the actual tracery of the window which contains them. The treatment of the figures, too, is dull. For the eight archbishops who form the bottom row, only two different patterns have been used, and in the row above the eleven apostles have been got into eight lights by making six of them squeeze, most uncomfortably, two in a niche.

The St. Stephen (Plate XX.) is from the sixth window in the south aisle, which seems to be of about the same date as the west windows and probably by the same glazier Robert. Instead of conforming to the design of the other windows in the aisle, he has filled it with three figures larger than life under tall canopies. It has likewise suffered much from eighteenth century restoration (the head, I think, is new), and has, besides, the same faults as the west windows. To me its chief interest is in the ornamentation of the saints' dalmatic, which affords the earliest example I know of the use of silver stain on blue glass, which may be seen in the ring-like ornaments on the blue stripes.

The parish churches of York contain a good deal of fourteenth as well as fifteenth century glass. The windows in the west end of the north aisle of All Saints', North Street, and the south aisle of St. Martin's, Micklegate, Plates XXI. and XXII., are not very easy to place with regard to the Cathedral work. My own opinion is that they are rather later and show a recovery in quality.

All Saints', North Street, and St. Martin's, Micklegate.

The canopies are as big as ever, but there is more taste and refinement in the drawing, both of the figures and ornaments, and more experience as well as taste in the use of the silver stain. At the same time, they contain later features, such as the attempt at perspective in the battlements above the canopy in Plate XXI., and in the brackets of a sort of balcony (not shown in the illustration) below. The curious device above the canopy in the window at St. Martin's (Plate XXII.) is, I imagine, the " merchant's mark " of the donor.

PLATE XXII.

ST. JOHN,
FROM EAST
WINDOW OF
SOUTH AISLE,
ST. MARTIN'S,
MICKLEGATE,
YORK
Fourteenth Century

XI

FOURTEENTH CENTURY GLASS
IN FRANCE

XI

FOURTEENTH CENTURY GLASS IN FRANCE

In France the change of style seems to have occurred very much at the same time as in England. There is some transitional work in St. Urbain at Troyes, to which Viollet-le-Duc gives the date 1295. This would make it a few years earlier in all probability than the Chapter-House at York, but the type of grisaille is rather earlier too, still consisting partly, like that at Exeter, of conventional foliage. The clerestory windows of the fine church of St. Pierre at Chartres, whatever their precise date, certainly mark the local change from the previous style. St. Pierre at Chartres.

The church had been begun as early as 1150, but its progress was slow and it was not completed till 1225, though the choir had been glazed in

1172.[1] The upper part of this choir was, however, pulled down in 1270, and rebuilt with large
traceried windows, filling all the wall space of the
clerestory. This again was not finished till 1310,
but this date probably refers to the completion of
the interior decoration which was always preceded
by the glazing of the windows. On the whole, I
think it is fairly safe to conclude that the choir
windows were done about 1300, or a little before.

The style is still that of the First Period but
modified, experimentally as it were, to suit new
conditions. Each window has four tall narrow
lights with tracery above, and every other light
is filled with two large figures placed one above
the other each in a medallion, which is squeezed
by the narrowness of the light into an elongated
form, while the space between the medallions is
filled in the old way with mosaic diaper of red
and blue. In compliance, however, with the
growing demand for more light in churches, the
other two lights in each window are filled entirely
with grisaille. This would give a lop-sided appearance to a single window, but seen together with

[1] Lasteyrie would have it that the existing windows represent this
glazing,—an extraordinary mistake for him to make,—but it is just
possible that they contain figures from the older windows.

only a slender shaft between window and window, they form a succession of alternate white and coloured vertical stripes all round the choir, an interesting and almost unique method of combining figure and grisaille. Altogether the clerestory windows may be considered as the very last work of the First Period already modified and influenced by the spirit of change that was in the air.

In the clerestory windows of the nave the change has already come about. Although in the richness of colouring there is still a reminiscence of the earlier style, yet the medallion has vanished, and everywhere, both over single figures and over subject panels, we find decorated canopies, not yet, however, of exaggerated proportions, and with a complete absence of yellow stain. In the general arrangement the same idea is seen as in the choir, but it has had to be adapted to a different form of window-opening. The nave is part of the original church of 1225, and the clerestory windows consist, like those of the Cathedral, of broad lights grouped in pairs, with a rose above each pair—the germ of tracery. Every alternate pair is entirely filled with small coloured scenes from the life of a saint,—no longer in medallions, but each framed under a small white canopy,—but the windows between

them have only a vertical stripe of colour down
the centre of each light containing two large
figures, one above the other, while the rest of the
light is filled with grisaille (Plate XXIII.).

The portrait of a certain abbot as donor enables
us to date these nave windows with fair accuracy
as about 1307–8, which makes them slightly later
than the Peter de Dene window in York Minster.
The grisaille is, however, of a distinctly earlier
type, having the background still cross-hatched,
but at Chartres one would expect the old traditions
to die hard.

Fourteenth
century glass
in Chartres
Cathedral.

There is fourteenth century work in the Cathedral,
which is interesting in its way. The window
given, about 1307–10, by "Geoffrey the Restorer,"
a canon whose "restoration" of the thirteenth
century windows was of a different kind to that
now in vogue, is the work of an archæologist and
an enthusiast for the older style and can hardly
be taken as typical. Very different is the strip
of glazing which Canon Thierry got leave, in 1328,
to insert in the foot of one of the big thirteenth
century windows in the south transept to light an
altar he had founded. Even for its date it is
remarkable, consisting, as it does, of figures (Canon
Thierry kneeling to the Virgin surrounded by

saints) executed entirely in white and silver stain, without any coloured glass, placed directly on a background of white and stain quarries. It is perhaps the first examples of this treatment of figures, and anything more hopelessly out of keeping with the deep and solemn colours above it can hardly be imagined, so that it is difficult to do it justice. An example of *coloured* figures placed directly on quarries is the Annunciation, which dates from 1350, in the south choir aisle, but it is not a very interesting group. The chapel of St. Piat contains some glass of the latter half of the century, but the treatment it has received prevents one forming an opinion of it.

The Cathedral of Evreux is rich in remains of Evreux. fourteenth century glass, which, like that at York, illustrates the progress of design during the century, the windows being of all dates from the opening of the fourteenth century till well on in the fifteenth. The earliest are those in the choir chapels, some of which are of about the same date as the Merton College glass, which, indeed, they at once call to mind. As at Merton, small coloured panels containing figures under low canopies are made to decorate long lights of grisaille. For the most part, as at Merton, the

figures consist of donors in the outer lights,
kneeling to their patron saints in the inner ones,
though occasionally one finds subjects, such as
the part of a Life of St. Martin in one of the
northern chapels.   One of the chapels in the apse
is remarkable for the charming use of heraldry
in the border.   The windows contain figures of
the Count of Evreux kneeling to the Virgin.   His
arms are the lilies of France with a bend "com-
ponèe" of argent and gules, and the fleur-de-lis
and the bend are repeated alternately all the way
up the border, on a ground of blue, with delightful
effect.

Later than these is the Harcourt window, the
earliest apparently of those in the clerestory, which
must date from between 1310 and 1327, though
I am inclined to think it is nearer the later date.
Here again one has the arrangement, so characteristic of the fourteenth century, of kneeling donors
in the outer lights and their patron saints in the
inner,—the first idea in nearly every fourteenth
century window is the safety of the donor's soul,—
but here the coloured panels are placed at the
very bottom of the window, with grisaille above,
an arrangement which one finds again in later
work at Rouen.   It has the advantage of bringing

the figures nearer the eye, but as a design it is hardly happy.

The fine church of St. Ouen at Rouen is very rich in fourteenth century glass of the first half of the century. The oldest, perhaps, is in the clerestory windows, which afford another example of the practice found, I think, earlier in France than in England, of placing figures directly on a background of quarries (Plate XXIV.). From the small amount of stain used I do not think they are likely to be later than 1330, though the queer little pedestal with its ogival arch does not look a very early feature.

St. Ouen at Rouen.

Rather later than these are the immense windows in the choir aisles, of which Plate XXV. is an example. In comparing them to those in York Minster, they seem to me to come, in point of development, between the aisle windows of the nave and the west windows, but are far better than the latter; yet, although there is hardly a detail in them which cannot be found in an earlier form at Merton College or York, they have, nevertheless, a character all their own, a hint of growing divergence between the two schools. The subject of this particular window is the Life of St. Gervais, but it is such an un-

important detail in the design as to be hardly
worth mentioning, the real interest of the windows
being their planning and ornament. They are
planned on precisely the same system as the
windows in Merton College chapel, in the choir
chapels at Evreux, and the aisles of York nave,
but the canopies are more highly developed, the
quarries are "true" quarries, and stain is much
more freely used. Plates XXVI.–XXX. show,
in detail, the use that has been made of it in the
grisaille borders and bosses of this window. Even
the canopies that are all yellow are, I fancy,
coloured with stain ; but the artist has been alive
to the danger of too much yellow in the window,
and has made every other canopy white, merely
touched with stain, a form which in time was
to supersede the other altogether. If you compare the little figure from one of these canopies
in Plate XXX. with the little border figures from
Peter de Dene's window at York, you will see
how the work is beginning to lose the mosaic
character it had inherited from the previous centuries. The grisaille patterns, as well as the
borders, show descent from, or at least common
origin with, those of York and Merton—you
can find that central stem with a wavy line on

LAWRENCE B. SAINT   APRIL 12, 1914

PLATE XXIII.

ST. BARNABAS,
FROM
CLERESTORY
OF NAVE OF
ST. PIERRE,
CHARTRES
Early Fourteenth
Century

PLATE XXIV.

ST. LUKE,
FROM CHOIR
CLERESTORY OF
ST. OUEN'S,
ROUEN

Fourteenth Century

it in both; but there is a subtle difference in the Rouen work—a little more grace, and more care that the foliage shall not only decorate the whole space of white, but form a symmetrical pattern on each individual quarry, a tendency which, however, may also be found in English work towards the end of the century.

Of later fourteenth century work there is not very much in France. The country was devastated by war, and there can have been little money or heart left for painted windows. Whichever side of the channel the style of the early four-teenth century originated, it is quite certain that the next great movement came from England.

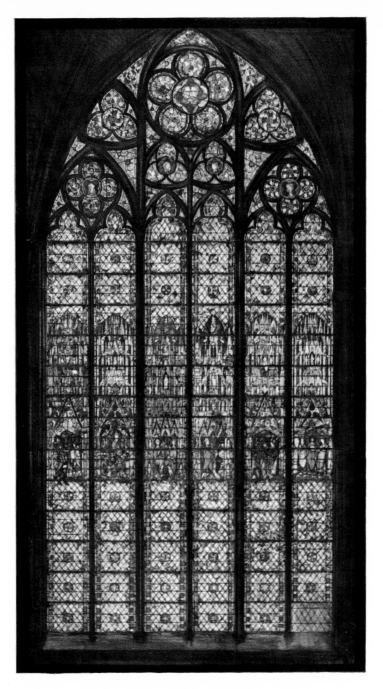

PLATE XXV.   WINDOW WITH LIFE OF ST. GERVAIS,
FROM SOUTH CHOIR AISLE, ST. OUEN'S, ROUEN
Fourteenth Century

XII

LATE FOURTEENTH CENTURY GLASS IN ENGLAND

(TRANSITIONAL—GLOUCESTER AND THE WORK OF THE WINCHESTER SCHOOL)

PLATE XXVI.   GRISAILLE PATTERN AND BOSS FROM PLATE XXV

LAWRENCE & SAINT
AUGT. 1911

PLATE XXVII.   BOSSES, FROM PLATE XXV

XII

LATE FOURTEENTH CENTURY GLASS IN ENGLAND

(TRANSITIONAL—GLOUCESTER AND THE WORK OF THE WINCHESTER SCHOOL)

An interesting thing about the design of stained glass in the fourteenth century is that it never stands still, but changes more rapidly than at any other period in its history. At Gloucester, not more than from ten to twenty years after the latest of the windows I have been describing, the great east window of the Cathedral was filled with glass, which already faintly foreshadows the change into the style of the succeeding period.

The Severn valley is rich in glass of the fourteenth century, the work of a school which may have had its headquarters at Gloucester, where, in later times, at all events, there were important

197

glass-works, which may still be seen in seventeenth century views of the city.

The fourteenth century glass at Shrewsbury, Tewkesbury, and Wells is all of this school, and differs in many little ways from the work at York, among which are the frequency of the ogival arch and gable in the canopies, and, at Wells, the presence of foliated brackets which support the figures. Whether the work in Bristol Cathedral also belongs to it I am not quite prepared to say.

The east window of Gloucester Cathedral.

I have no space, however, to describe these windows, and must return to the east window of Gloucester Cathedral which is later in style than any of them. Winston, who has given it the same careful study that he had devoted to the Peter de Dene window at York, points out that the coats of arms in it are all those of nobles who took part in the Campaign of Crècy in 1346 and deduces that the date of the window is not later than 1350, whereas Westlake thinks it cannot be earlier than 1360. In either case it is remarkable. To begin with, the tracery of this immense window, the second largest in England, is pure Perpendicular, and the earliest important example of it. The glass, on the other hand, in its architectural detail, style of drawing, and material used, belongs almost wholly to the Second or Decorated Period, and it is mainly in its planning and general colour scheme that we find a hint of approaching change. The perpendicular mullions and horizontal transoms divide the great window, which is slightly bowed outwards to give its strength, into a series of horizontal rows of narrow lights one above the other, fourteen lights in a row, each light being about two feet wide and from six to nine feet high. The lower tiers (and originally this was true of the tracery as well) are filled with quarries, and the upper one of these, the first that extends all across the window,—for the entrance to the Lady Chapel makes a gap below it,—is decorated with the splendid row of coats of arms already mentioned. Above this each light, row upon row, contains a figure under a canopy, the side shafts of which extend into the light above and support the canopy there, while the central pinnacle also extends upwards past the transom and expands into a flat-topped pedestal which carries the figure above. Figure and canopy are white, their whiteness only emphasised by touches of yellow stain, and relieved against a coloured background. The background of the two central columns of lights is ruby, that of the column on each side blue, and the next ruby again and so on alternately. Thus the general effect is of a white pattern on a background that is striped vertically with alternate red and blue. It is this simple but effective colour scheme that gives the window its resemblance in effect to Perpendicular glass; but there are other features— the complete absence of borders, the pedestals that carry the figures (which are first found at Wells), and the decoration of the quarries—which all indicate the coming change. The quarries, where the original ones remain, still have the " trellis " pattern, but instead of the continuous flowing pattern of foliage running through them each quarry has a sort of star pattern in the middle of it, stained yellow, a design much more common in the fifteenth than in the fourteenth century. This placing of quarries at the foot of the windows and in the tracery has its origin, of course, in the old fourteenth century arrangement of a horizontal stripe or stripes of figure and canopy work on a ground of grisaille.

The subject of the window is the enthronement of the virgin surrounded by apostles, saints, and angels; the same subject as that of the west window of York Minster which it was probably

meant to, and certainly does, surpass. The figures
themselves, however, still suffer from the conventionality and affectation of the period, and it was
not for twenty years more that there was to be a
change in that quarter as well.

It was in 1380, or soon after, that new life came
into the art through the piety and enterprise of
William of Wykeham, whose influence may be
compared to that of Abbot Suger in the twelfth
century, and the genius of his master glazier,
Thomas. Of the latter we only know his name
from the portrait of himself which he put in the
windows of Winchester College Chapel (now, alas !
only modern copies of the originals), with the
inscription " Thomas operator ist. vitri," but his
hand is easily recognizable not only at Winchester,
and in the three original lights from thence now in
South Kensington Museum, but in the glorious set
of windows in the antechapel of New College at
Oxford.

William of
Wykeham
and Thomas
the Glazier.

There had been no such work as this last done
since the best days of the thirteenth century.
Here, once again, one finds the art used as a means
of emotional expression not only in the deep and
solemn harmonies of colour that strike one with a
thrill on entering the building, but in the treat-

New College
antechapel.

ment of the subjects themselves, in which the artist breaks completely away from the conventionalism of the preceding period.

The antechapel ot New College, a graceful piece of Early Perpendicular, is really, like that at Merton, a cross transept at the west end of the Chapel, forming a T of which the antechapel is the head, having windows on all its four sides— two on the east, on either side of the entrance to the Chapel proper, two on the north, one on the south, and three on the west. The glass of the great central west window was taken out to make room for Jervais' smudgy rendering in muddy browns and yellows of Sir Joshua Reynolds' famous Virtues. I am not concerned with this but with the other windows, which contain, though some of the lights are evidently out of their order, the original glazing which William of Wykeham placed here when he built the Chapel, between 1380 and 1386.

The design of the windows is a very simple one. The horizontal transom divides each window into two equal tiers of four, or, in the eastern windows, six, lights with tracery above. Each light is filled with a figure standing on a pedestal and under a canopy, both canopy and pedestal being white, enriched with touches of yellow stain, relieved against a background which is, or was, blue and red in alternate lights, the colour of the background inside the canopy being counterchanged with the colour outside. From this arrangement and from the presence of the pedestal I think the artist had seen both Wells and the east windows of Gloucester Cathedral, but the architecture of his canopies is of a fantastic kind peculiar to this school and unlike anything in glass of the styles which preceded and followed it, but based to some extent on the stone canopies of the late fourteenth century, such as those on the screen of the west front of Exeter Cathedral. The most noticeable feature in them is the number of queer rounded turrets with pepper-box tops, modelled in relief. Indeed for their solidity, as well as for their violent and untrue perspective, these canopies have more in common with those introduced at Fairford a hundred years later, when the continental influence was coming in, than with the typical canopy of English Perpendicular.

The canopies.

From the large amount of space that is occupied by the canopy work, the general effect of these windows is rather a white one (though white in all old work is a relative term, the white in this case consisting really of a delicate play of greenish, yellowish, and pure white continually contrasted), and the most beautiful to my mind are those in which, as in the windows on the north side which face one on entering, the figures themselves are almost entirely covered with a coloured mantle which makes a broad splash of distinctive colour in the middle of each light.

The eastern windows.

Although all the windows conform to the same general design, those on the east side, on each side of the entrance to the Chapel proper, seem to me to be by a different hand, and were probably done first. They contain or contained originally no colours but red and blue, and the drawing of the figures has much of the conventionalism of the earlier fourteenth century work. The upper tier consists of the twelve apostles, and the lower is believed to have contained the figure of the crucified Christ with His mother and St. John on either side, repeated four times. The figures of Christ have all been destroyed and replaced by figures from elsewhere, perhaps from the destroyed west window; but three figures of the Virgin and three of St. John remain, though it was only in 1900 that they were replaced in what I have little doubt were their original positions. It may, of

PLATE XXVIII.

BORDERS
FROM
PLATE XXV

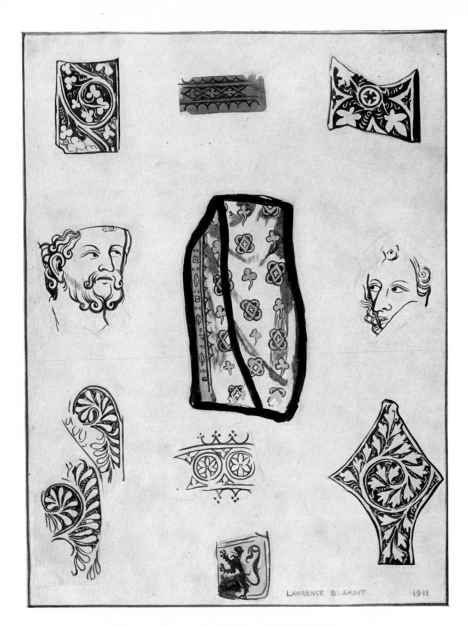

LAWRENCE B. SAINT 1911

PLATE XXIX. DETAILS, FROM PLATE XXV

course, be that these windows are by the same artist as the others, but done before he had quite found himself or emancipated himself from the conventionalities of his predecessors, for he has infused a certain amount of life into the old forms; and the "Mater Dolorosa," in spite of her conventional S-like pose, is a tender and pathetic figure.

There is, however, no trace of this conventionality in the other windows, quaint though the drawing may be, and in the colour of them the artist has fairly "let himself go." I know of no better piece of "colour music" in the world than is afforded by the double tier of prophets and patriarchs which occupy the two northern windows which face one on entering—deep rich purple of many shades, warm green, slaty-blue, brown, and a splendid blood-red ruby with a great deal of variety in it; the changes are rung on these in the mantles, hats, and shoes of the figures, while the reds and blues of the backgrounds form a connecting link between them all. A pretty detail is the powdering of the backgrounds to the figures in all the windows with the initials of the personage represented, in white Lombardic letters surmounted by little gold crowns. The drawing is, I admit, quaint,—Thomas was not a great draughtsman

The colouring.

even for his time; far from it,—but it is always big, masculine, and expressive, with a strong feeling for decorative line. To copy the scrolls which twist and flutter round the prophets in the upper tier is in itself a lesson in design.

Eve.   Perhaps nowhere is his originality of conception so well shown as in the figure of Eve, in the northern west window. Instead of representing her, as nearly every other artist has done to the best of his ability, as a graceful nude, he has given us a peasant woman of his own time, spinning with a distaff and spindle. I do not know that he has even tried to make her pretty, and in the simple drawing of the folds of her colourless dress he has managed to suggest that it is of coarse thick stuff. She is neither nymph nor princess but the sharer of man's daily drudgery. In looking at her one is unavoidably reminded of the lines which Wat Tyler's followers had sung only a year or two before:—

> When Adam delved and Eve span,
> Who was then the gentleman?

The little upright tracery lights are filled with angels, but in the summit of the northern east window is a small figure of William of Wykeham kneeling before his Saviour, who shows His wounds.

This and the mutilated inscription at the base of each light, "Orate pro Willelmo de Wykeham, Episcopo Wynton, fundatore istius collegii," is all there is to tell of the donor. There was a new spirit abroad; no longer were the portrait and arms of the patron allowed to usurp half, or, as at Tewkesbury, the whole of a church window, nor in England, at all events till the end of the fifteenth century, was the practice again revived to quite the same extent.

These windows mark the second of the great periodic impulses in stained glass, which I spoke of at the beginning of the book. Only the second, I consider, for though there had been many changes in style since the twelfth century, each had meant, on the whole, a loss of beauty rather than a gain, whereas now we find a sudden infusion of new life into the art, which did not in England lose its force for fifty or sixty years to come, and produced a new style, the style of the Third Period. To me these windows are one of the great art treasures of the world, yet as I lately sat there all through a long spring afternoon, party after party of visitors, many of them people educated enough, one would think, to know better, came in to gaze awe-struck at Sir Joshua's muddy brown Virtues, and left without a glance at the glorious colour harmonies which surrounded them.

Of other work of Thomas the Glazier and his school—the Winchester school, as Mr. Westlake calls it—little but fragments remain, unless one counts a window in the south aisle of the Lady Chapel of York Minster, the third from the east, which somewhat resembles their work and represents just about the same stage in development.   William of Wykeham's next great work was the founding of Winchester College in 1387, and in what remains of its glass the hand of Thomas can be clearly seen. But, alas! in the early nineteenth century they took out the old glass and substituted modern copies ; it was their method of restoration in those days.   The old glass seems to have been the perquisite of the glazier, and three of the lights, after various peregrinations,—spending eight years in a window of St. Mary's, Shrewsbury,—have found their way to South Kensington Museum where they may still be seen.   In style they are very like the north, west, and south windows at New College, and quite obviously by the same hand, though perhaps the canopies, at least in one case, show a very slight progress towards the regular Perpendicular type.   The material seems to me much

Winchester College.

PLATE XXX.   ANGELS IN CANOPY WORK OF PLATE XXV

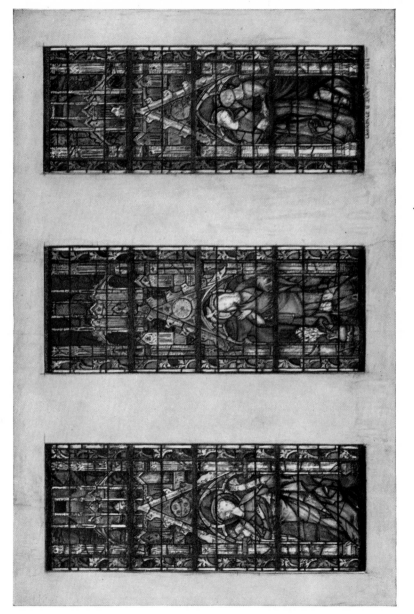

PLATE XXXI.   THE ANNUNCIATION, FROM ST. OUEN'S, ROUEN

Fourteenth Century

the same as at New College, but for some reason the coloured glass is much more pitted by the weather and consequently obscured, though the white, perhaps from a different shop, is in splendid preservation.

The great west window of Winchester Cathedral Winchester contains fragments and a few whole figures of very Cathedral. similar work, and there are others in the side windows of the nave. William of Wykeham's will, made in 1403, leaves money for the glazing of the Cathedral windows "beginning from the west at the first window of the new work done by him," which sounds as if the west end had been already glazed. Indeed the fragments there are more like the eastern windows (the earliest, if I am right) in New College ante-chapel, while in the fragments that remain in the side windows of the nave the later hand can be traced, though the tendency in the canopies of these is to assimilate gradually to the regular Perpendicular type which by this time had been developed elsewhere.

Winston thinks the west window of the Cathedral may have been glazed in the time of William of Wykeham's predecessor, Bishop Edington, in which case it is not unlikely that it and the east windows of the antechapel at New College were the work of Thomas's master, whose style was further developed and improved by Thomas himself.

14

XIII
THE STYLE OF THE THIRD PERIOD

PLATE XXXII.

WINDOW IN
ST. BARTHOLOMEW'S
CHAPEL, ST. OUEN'S,
ROUEN
Fourteenth Century

PLATE XXXIII.   DETAILS, FROM ST. OUEN'S, ROUEN
Fourteenth Century

XIII

THE STYLE OF THE THIRD PERIOD

A NOTABLE feature of the fifteenth century is the divergence which takes place in it between the styles of English and French stained glass. Although in some respects they develop along parallel lines the two no longer form, as they did almost to the end of the fourteenth century, one school. The Hundred Years' War has done its work, and produced a separation of spirit for which the world has, perhaps, been the poorer ever since.

Indeed for the first half of the fifteenth century, during which the best of the English work was done, the quantity of stained glass produced in France seems to have been almost negligible, and a comparison of the conditions of the two countries is a sufficient explanation of this fact. While England was becoming rich and prosperous and developing her foreign trade, France was laid

Divergence between English and French schools.

213

waste by war and struggling to free herself from the
foreigner who had beaten her down.   It was not
till the English had been finally expelled, and
France had emerged from the struggle a stronger
State than she had ever been before, that the art
revived ; and when it did so it owed little, as is not
surprising, to English influence, but on the other
hand began to feel, almost at once, the influence of
the Continental schools of painting.

In England, on the other hand, in spite of the
quarrels of the nobles and the rival claimants to
the throne, the middle class were steadily growing
wealthy and powerful.   The wool trade was bringing a great deal of money into the country, and the
result is still seen not only in the number and size
of Perpendicular churches that were built, but in
the immense output of stained glass that took
place.   The fifteenth century, indeed, was by far
the most prolific period in the history of English
stained glass, and, in spite of four hundred years
of destruction, vast quantities of it still remain.

General character- istics of the English style.

The general characteristics which distinguish
the English style in glass in the Third Period—
the " Perpendicular " style—are as follows :—

(1) The type of canopy.

(2) The increased amount of white in figure and

canopy work, with the delicate and accomplished use of silver stain.

(3) The more advanced style of drawing.

(4) The abandonment of natural form in ornament.

(5) The supersession of all other forms of grisaille ornament by regular quarries.

(6) The material used.

(1) *The Type of Canopy.*—Although in the The canopy fifteenth, as in the fourteenth century, figures were occasionally placed directly on a background of white quarries, as may be seen at York, in the clerestory of St. Martin's - le - Grand, and in the transepts of the Minster, the fifteenth century artists showed no signs of wishing to abandon the canopy.

It was a curious freak of fate that imposed the canopy upon stained-glass designers and made it a *sine quâ non* for two hundred years.   It has certain obvious advantages, it is true.   It conveniently filled the head of the light, and its upright lines and pinnacles repeated those of the surrounding architecture and made the window part of it; but the imitation of a stone niche in glass is hard to justify on abstract grounds, and it is difficult now to understand the enthusiasm which, as soon as it was introduced, made its adoption so universal that, with few exceptions, the artists of the day seemed unable to conceive of a single figure or a set of subject panels otherwise than surmounted by a bewildering mass of crockets and pinnacles. It is true that in the hands of mediæval craftsmen, in England at least, there was no attempt, as there was later, at literal imitation of stonework; the canopy was rather ornament with an architectural motif, and as such possessed beauty; but I cannot help thinking that if they had never adopted it they would have evolved some other ornamental form which, while serving the same purposes, would have been more strictly in accordance with the rules of sound art, and might have given more room for the play of individual fancy.

Though, however, the English fifteenth century craftsmen did not abandon the canopy, they profoundly modified it and made it far more pliant and adaptable. Plates XXXIV. and XXXV. from York will give a better idea of the canopies of the early fifteenth century than any description. It will be seen that the single overpowering crocketted gable and wall-sided tower of the fourteenth century has disappeared, and in its place we have a

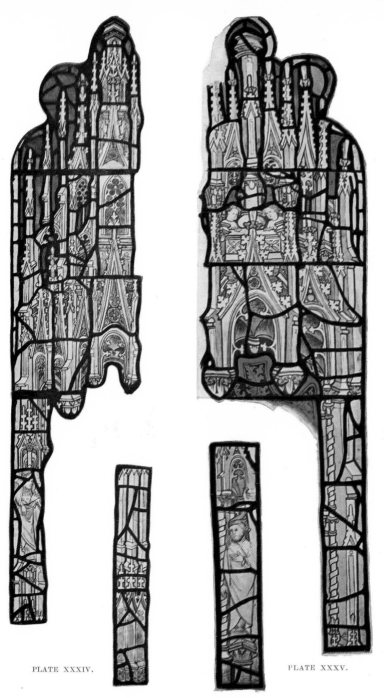

PLATE XXXIV.   PLATE XXXV.

CANOPIES FROM ALL SAINTS', NORTH STREET, YORK
Fifteenth Century

froth of pinnacles, windows, buttresses and niches
all in white and yellow stain, on a background of
colour. The earlier attempt at modelling the
canopies in the round, which is seen in the work of
the Winchester school, had been abandoned, and
although every little shaft has its light and dark
side delicately distinguished, this counts for little
except to diversify the surface, the forms being
expressed principally in strong and simple outline.
The extent to which this simplification of outline
was carried may be seen in the little crocketted
pinnacles, such as those at the bottom of Plate
XXXIV., which are characteristic of all English
work of the time. There is, as you may see, no
attempt to draw or model the foliation of the
crockets, which are simply knobs outlined in the
flat with a thick black line. This method is the
salvation of English Perpendicular work, and
shows the thorough understanding on the part of
our craftsmen of the technical problem. In French
work later on in the century, and in much modern
pseudo-Gothic work, the attempt is made to express the canopy work in fine lines and delicate
modelling, which, in the result, appears confused
and indistinct, and too weak for the leading and
for the coloured figure work it encloses.

(2) *The Increased Amount of White used.*—Not only is the canopy white, but there is also as a rule a good deal of white in the figures within it, which are generally relieved against a diapered flat background of colour. Just one figure at New College has the brown-pink flesh colour, and that is its last appearance. Everywhere else one finds white used, the hair, in the case of women and young men, being stained yellow. This large increase in the use of white glass was accompanied, and indeed made

The skilful use of silver stain.

possible, by a most delicate and skilful use of the yellow silver stain. This operation, of all others in stained-glass work, calls for the greatest exercise of taste and judgment as well as skill on the part of the craftsman,—*experto crede,*—and in its use the English workers of the first three-quarters of the fifteenth century stand unrivalled.

This use of white in the figures and canopies rendered unnecessary the old fourteenth century plan of dividing the window up into alternate panels of grisaille and colour, and this is abandoned.

Loss of mosaic character.

Another result is the loss of the essentially mosaic character of the older windows. So much could now be expressed with stain and brown enamel on one piece of glass that, although the pieces used were still comparatively small, it was no longer

PLATE XXXVI. NICHOLAS BLACKBURN AND HIS WIFE,
FROM EAST WINDOW OF ALL SAINTS', NORTH STREET, YORK
Fifteenth Century

necessary to surround every form with a lead as a matter of course. Plate XXXVI. is a good instance of this. The green-striped background to the figures is the work of the restorer and was probably once blue, as in Plate XXXVII., and this and the red mantle surcoat and shield are the only forms that it was absolutely necessary to lead in separately. It is true that, either for emphasis or from habit, the artist has outlined the man's knees in lead; but he need not have done so, and it would indeed have been easier not to. In the next plate (Plate XXXVII.) the leading on the white takes very little account of the drawing.

Out of these conditions then arose a wholly new attitude towards the leading. Hitherto the disposition of the lead-work had followed naturally and inevitably from the design—the artist drew in lead, so to speak, merely supplementing it with the finer painted line; whereas now the leads had, in part at least, to be so arranged as not to interfere with the drawing, or only to emphasize it when needed, a matter requiring much more thought. A comparison of either of the above plates with Plate IV. will illustrate the difference. Hence we find a gradual tendency to use larger pieces of glass and fewer leads (the latter being sometimes concealed behind the iron-work), till by the end of the century the jewel-like quality of the early glass is a thing wholly lost and forgotten.

The method of drawing.

(3) *The more Advanced Style of Drawing.*—The older conventions in drawing had, as we have seen, become outgrown and abandoned, and all through the last part of the fourteenth century there is a steady struggle for a more advanced method of expression. At the beginning of the fifteenth century, drawing, in England at least, crystallized once more into a convention satisfying to the mind of the time, which left the artist free to tell his story. Plates XXXIX. to XLIII. are examples of it as found at York, and Plate XLIV. from Canterbury does not greatly differ in method. The drawing still depends chiefly on line work, but the line work is far finer than before and is used

Matt shading.

to express modelling with the help of the matt shading. This last is the form of shading which has survived to modern times, and is done by laying a flat semi-transparent coat or "matt" of enamel over the whole surface of the glass, and, when it is dry, and before it is fired, brushing out graduated lights and half tones with a small stiff hog's-hair brush. Sometimes, but not always, the matt was stippled when wet, as may be seen in Plate XLII.

PLATE XXXVII. PRIEST, FROM " ACTS OF MERCY " WINDOW, ALL SAINTS',
NORTH STREET, YORK
Fifteenth Century

PLATE XXXVIII. KNEELING DONORS, FROM " ACTS OF MERCY " WINDOW, ALL SAINTS',
NORTH STREET, YORK

Fifteenth Century

In later times the matt shading was, and sometimes still is, abused in the attempt to give
modelling in high relief by its means alone, a
method which results in the loading of the glass
with opaque muddy brown, while the modelling
becomes untrue with changing lights. This, however, was hardly done within the limits of the
period I am writing about in this book, in which
the drawing of form is still principally dependent
on line work, and is merely helped and softened
with the matt.

The figures themselves in contrast to those of
the previous period are rather short and ungraceful,
but, in the best work at least, very much alive.
The quaint nose of which Plate XLII. is an
extreme type is curiously universal throughout
English work of the time, and was, I suppose, the
accepted type of beauty.

(4) *The Abandonment of Natural Plant Forms
in Ornament.*—The natural plant forms, which were
so universally used in fourteenth century ornament,
were abruptly abandoned at the beginning of the
fifteenth. Their place is taken, in the diapered
backgrounds to the figures, by a curious long
serrated leaf, rather like certain kinds of seaweed,
which may be seen in Plates XXXVII. and

The type of figure.

Forms used in the ornament.

XXXVIII. Borders become less frequent, and
when they occur generally consist of a leaf of
something the same sort, in white and stain,
wrapping round a central stem, sometimes with
and sometimes without a coloured background.
Later on, the conventional pomegranate pattern is
occasionally introduced in vestments and hangings,
but it is the exception for coloured garments to
be ornamented except with an edging. White
garments are sometimes powdered with little
devices in yellow stain, as in Plate XXXIX.
The edgings to bishops' copes are often of white
set with coloured jewels, which are sometimes let
into the middle of a piece of glass without its
being cut across—a *tour de force* of glazing very
difficult to accomplish and not worth the trouble
when done.

(5) *Supersession of Other Forms of Grisaille by
Regular Quarries.*—The " bulged " quarries disappear by the middle of the fourteenth century
and the ordinary straight-sided, diamond-shaped
quarry is henceforth the rule. By the end of
the century the continuous flowing pattern running
through them is abandoned also. There had been
a tendency towards the end, as may be seen in
Plate XXVI., for the pattern to be so disposed

that a flower, or other feature, was repeated in the middle of each quarry—in a transitional window at York, which I have referred to elsewhere, there is a continuous pattern with a bird in the centre of each quarry perching upon a branch of it.   In the fifteenth century the connecting pattern was left out, and quarries are decorated solely by a little device in the centre of each.   Sometimes these are purely conventional, but often they are the occasion for delightful exercise of fancy on the artist's part and form an exception to the general rule of the disuse of natural ornament. Birds, insects, flowers, and leaves are used, as well as heraldic devices and monograms, all expressed very simply in firm pure line work touched with the yellow stain.

(6) *The Material used.*—At the beginning of the fifteenth century there is a very marked change in the material used.   It becomes thinner and flatter — sometimes very thin indeed — and the colour is more even.   Thirteenth century "ruby," seen edgeways, reveals itself as composed, for nearly, if not quite, half its thickness, of alternate minute layers of red and white, the rest of the thickness being white.   It has been thought that to this is due the wonderful luminous quality of the

The change in material.

early ruby.   Gradually the number of these layers are reduced till at the beginning of the fifteenth century the red is all concentrated into one layer on the surface.   This is the "flashed" glass referred **Flashed ruby.** to at the beginning of the book, and one soon begins to find instances of ornament chipped out of it.   The lion on the red shield in Plate XXXVI. has, I think, been got in this way, and a later instance may be seen in Plate L. in the girdle of the prophet Hosea on the right.

The rich blues of earlier times are replaced by a more sober greyish blue, which, however, is a very effective colour in glass.   The colours are not perfectly flat tints, for there are gradations in them, but the streaky, crumbly quality of the early glass is gone.   The craftsman was beginning to rely for quality less on the glass itself than on what he put on it.

XIV

FIFTEENTH CENTURY GLASS
AT YORK

XIV

FIFTEENTH CENTURY GLASS
AT YORK

THE very well-defined and distinctive style I have described, which became universal in English fifteenth century work, and which, from the architecture with which it is associated, we call Perpendicular, was not, I think, evolved by the Winchester School, although no doubt they influenced it. Where it began must always be something of a mystery, but some work in the east window of Exeter Cathedral is very suggestive in this connection.

This window, glazed originally at the beginning of the fourteenth century, was enlarged and re-built with Perpendicular tracery in 1390–91 through the munificence of one of the canons, Henry Blake-born ; and in 1392 Robert Lyen, glazier, citizen of Exeter, and master glazier to the Cathedral, was commissioned to adapt the old glass to its new

Lyen's work at Exeter.

227

setting, adding what was necessary of his own work to fill the space. Robert Lyen's work is easily to be distinguished from the earlier work (which, besides that of 1302, includes four figures of about 1340–50, which he may have brought from other windows to fill up with). It consists of six figures, of which only three are under canopies of Lyen's time, and of a row, across the bottom, of short double-arched canopies enclosing coats of arms of past bishops of Exeter. The drawing is about equal to that of the Winchester School, but the canopies, with their multitude of crocketted pinnacles in strong outline, are far nearer to the regular Perpendicular type, such as we find at York, than anything that was being done by the Winchester School at that date.

Was the work of Robert Lyen an example of a style which had become general throughout the west, and of which the influence extended as far as Coventry? For in 1405 John Thornton of Coventry was commissioned to fill with stained glass the huge east windows of the new choir of York Minster, and this is the earliest existing window, of which the date is known, in which the Perpendicular style in glass has taken definite form.

This great window is the glory of English

stained glass.   It is 78 feet high from top to
bottom, and below the great mass of Perpendicular tracery, which fills the mighty pointed
arch of it, there are the three tiers of lower lights
divided by horizontal transoms, with nine lights
in every tier.   Each of these lights measures 3
feet 6 inches across, and is divided again by the
thick iron frame-bars into roughly square panels,
each of which contains a subject from the Bible.
The canopy work which, in the hands of a fourteenth century artist, would have filled half the
window space with its towering spires, is here reduced to a small many-pinnacled canopy just filling
the head of each light (where it would have been
an awkward shape for a subject), a narrow shafting
forming a border down the side, and a very shallow
flat arch dividing each subject from the one above.
There has been no question here of eking out a
poverty of ideas; on the contrary, the artist's aim
seems rather to have been to get as much space as
possible for the expression of them.

The east window of York Minster.

There are one hundred and seventeen of these
subject panels.   Thornton would seem to have
begun at the top with the idea of telling the whole
story of the Old Testament, or perhaps that of the
entire Bible, but by the time he had finished the

upper tier, which contains three rows of panels, as compared with five in each tier below, and carried the story as far as the death of Absalom, he, or more probably his clients, seem to have changed their minds, for the rest of the window, with the exception of the bottom row panels, is devoted to the illustration of the Apocalypse, beginning with the torture of St. John under Domitian and his banishment to Patmos.

John Thornton was a greater draughtsman than Thomas of Winchester, and the portrayal of these scenes is far in advance, from the pictorial point of view, of anything that had been done in glass up to that time. Here again one feels, as in the best days of the Early Period, that one can take pleasure in the actual technique of the painting, but it is a different technique to that of the Early Period. The line work is still wonderfully precise and expressive, but it is more delicate than before, and is helped by delicate modelling in "matt shading," while the drawing itself is in a much more modern convention. It is, indeed, the first example in stained glass of a style of drawing which was to hold the field in England till nearly the end of the century, and to John Thornton is due, probably, the credit of its introduction.

PLATE XXXIX.

FIGURE FROM
" VISITING THE
PRISONERS,"
IN " ACTS OF MERCY "
WINDOW,
ALL SAINTS',
NORTH STREET,
YORK
Fifteenth Century

PLATE XL. SMALL FIGURES IN WHITE AND STAIN, FROM ALL SAINTS',
NORTH STREET, YORK

Fifteenth Century

As a colourist, however, John Thornton is even greater. This window stands almost alone in England, if not in Europe, for the way in which colour is made use of as a means of expression. Elsewhere in York the successors of John Thornton seem to have been content with a merely decorative distribution of red, blue, and silver stain in their subjects, but here each scene has its appropriate colour scheme, the creation of fishes, for instance, being a lovely harmony of blue and silvery white, while the scenes in Eden are a glory of spring-like greens and gold.

Its colouring.

The necessary element of strength in the construction of this huge window, which, at Gloucester was, as we have seen, obtained by building the whole window on the plan of a bow, is here provided by doubling the mullions below the second transom. An inner set has been constructed between three and four feet on the inside of those which sustain the glass, being connected with them by little flying arches and so acting as buttresses to them. This double set of mullions carries a gallery along its top at the level of the upper transom, while another runs across the base of the window, and from these it is possible to study the upper and lower tiers of lights at close

Its construction.

quarters. Unfortunately access to these galleries is nowadays only granted as a great favour, but for those that can obtain it, it is well worth the trouble, for it is only from this position that the pages of this vast picture-book can be studied, and its story unravelled. Indeed I think the only adverse criticism that can be made of John Thornton's work is to question the artistic wisdom of putting so much beautiful work, on such a small scale,—for the delicate drawing and finish of the work is wonderful,—in a position in which it was invisible to the ordinary observer below. Perhaps John Thornton did not realize how small his panels would look,—panels three and a half feet square seem a fair size when you are working at them,— and no doubt access to the galleries was freer then than now; but a thirteenth century artist would not have made the mistake.[1]

Yet the architectural effect of the whole is little, if at all, the worse for it. The smallness of the panels only increases one's sense of the size of the window and gives the glass a jewel-like quality. It is all a twinkle of beautiful colour. Neither have the repairs effected by the eighteenth century

[1] Perhaps it is unfair to blame Thornton, for in the contract he undertakes to work "secundum ordinationem Decani et Capituli."

glaziers hurt it much—pieces of clear coloured glass put in to fill up holes, and on which the glazier has usually scratched his name and the date with his diamond.   Rather, I think, these tiny touches of pure colour (for they used quite a good blue) add to it and give it a quality.

What does detract from its beauty is the dirty quarry glazing which has been put outside it to protect it.   Beautiful as the window still is, quite a third of its beauty of light and colour has been sacrificed by this means.

There is some glass in the Lady Chapel which A transi-seems older than the east window.   I have tional already alluded to the third window from the window. east in the south aisle which represents a stage of development corresponding to the earlier work of the Winchester School in the west window of Winchester Cathedral and the east windows of New College antechapel.   The three lights contain three figures, St. Edward the Confessor between St. James and St. John the Evangelist, unless the former figure is also St. John appearing to the king as a pilgrim, as in the well-known story.   Below are small scenes of the Massacre of the Innocents, Christ among the Doctors, and the Baptism in Jordan. The figures still have something of the S-like curve of the fourteenth century, but the canopies are white and of the transitional type. Perhaps the most interesting things in the window are the quarry panels at the bottom, which have a continuous flowing pattern of oak foliage running through the quarries, but with birds perching on it, so arranged that a bird comes in the centre of each quarry.

There is some similar glass to this in the clerestory, but, with this exception and that of a fourteenth century window in the south aisle which has evidently been moved from the nave, the rest of the glass in the choir and Lady Chapel is the work of the school which was either founded Thornton's by John Thornton at York, or at least profoundly successors. influenced by him. It seems probable to me that it was in their work, which is found not only in the Cathedral but also in most of the parish churches of York, that the Perpendicular style in glass finally crystallized into the form which, with minor local differences, became universal throughout England.

Details from their work may be seen in Plates XXXIV.-XLIII. In one respect, namely in colour, they did not, as I have said, follow John Thornton, limiting themselves, for some reason unknown, very much to ruby, blue, and yellow

PLATE XLI.   HEADS, FROM ALL SAINTS', NORTH STREET, YORK

Fifteenth Century

PLATE XLII.   HEAD, FROM ST. MICHAEL'S, SPURRIERGATE, YORK
Fifteenth Century

stain. Plate XXXVIII. is a good instance of their method (the background of Plate XXXVI., it must be remembered, is modern). The blue is of a greyish quality, quite different from that of early times, but pleasant, and with a good deal of variety in it; a blue-black was sometimes used, as in Plate XXXVII., for monks' dresses.

The only exception to this rule is a window in the south aisle of the Cathedral choir, which contains parts of a Jesse Tree, in which the blue A Jesse Tree. is combined with some very beautiful rich dark greens and a strong orange stain. Mr. Westlake thinks the glass is not York work at all. To me it seems not quite impossible that it is the work of John Thornton himself, the use of the deep orange stain in the east window being very similar. There is, however, no certainty of his authorship of any existing window but the east window. The glass in the Guildhall of Coventry is sometimes claimed for him, but I do not know of any evidence for it, and as it contains a portrait of Henry VI. as a grown man it can hardly be much earlier than 1440, thirty-five years later than the east window at York.

Next to the great east window, the most important windows in the choir are those which

The
St. William
and
St. Cuthbert
windows.

fill the two choir-transepts, and which tell the
histories respectively of St. William of York and
St. Cuthbert. They are only five lights wide, but
extend upwards to the full height of the church,
and have double tracery and galleries like the east
window. Except for their prevailing red and blue
colouring, their general design resembles that of
the east window, the whole window being divided,
in the same way, into a series of small square
subject panels with a short many-pinnacled canopy
just filling the head of each light. The St. Cuthbert window, however, has, in addition, a life-size
figure of the saint, which occupies two panels in
the middle of the window. The two windows are
evidently by the same hand, but the northern or
St. William window is a good deal the older,
having been presented, as it would seem from the
portraits it contains, by Baron Ros of Hamlake
about 1420, while the St. Cuthbert window cannot
have been given till after 1426, and probably
not till 1430 or later. No doubt, however, the
execution of the first window would occupy a
large part of the intervening time. Of the two,
I rather prefer the effect of the St. William
window, to which the larger amount of dark blue
in the monks' dresses gives greater depth and

richness, but the St. Cuthbert window shows perhaps more accomplishment in drawing. It is a fascinating occupation on a bright day to trace, with the aid of a strong field-glass, the stories unfolded in these rows upon rows of pictures in glass, to which a key may be found in monographs on the two windows, by the Rev. J. T. Fowler and his brother, published in the *Yorkshire Archæological Journal,* vols. iii.-iv.

More easily studied, because nearer to the eye, are the windows, again by the same hand, in the churches of St. Martin's, Coney Street, and All Saints', North Street. The former has a large west window containing a life-size figure of St. Martin, surrounded by small scenes from his life, the gift of a former vicar, Robert Semer, who has most obligingly recorded the date—1437—in an inscription. This would probably make it just a little later than the St. Cuthbert window, which its arrangement resembles. The glass at All Saints' is particularly interesting. The east window has three lights with large figures under canopies of the type shown in Plates XXXIV. and XXXV., which, though elaborate enough, have none of the unwieldiness of the fourteenth century type and are properly subordinate to the figures. These are

St. Martin's Coney Street.

All Saints', North Street.

St. Peter and St. Christopher (always a favourite
subject in England), and, between them, St. Anne,
teaching the Virgin to read. This last is a very
beautiful group; the Virgin, a graceful girlish
figure in white and yellow stain, with a wreath
of white flowers round her head, is pointing with
a short stick to the letters in a book held by her
mother, who wears a deep ruby mantle over a blue
dress, and a most curious red turban-like headdress [1]
with ermine stripes, which is one of the most
striking things in the window.

Below are the donors, Nicholas Blackburn, twice
Mayor of York, and his wife Margaret (Plate
XXXVI.), facing his son, also named Nicholas, and
his wife, also named Margaret. The window has
unfortunately been a good deal restored, and the
background to the Blackburns is modern and was,
I should think, originally blue. Modern, too, is
the vivid green of the younger Nicholas's cloak.
Margaret Blackburn, the elder, carries a book with
the words, "Domine, labia mea aperies et os
meum." The same verse occurs also, if I re-
member right, in a lady's hand at Selby Abbey.
Were Yorkshire women, one wonders, so very silent?

[1] This is thought by some to be a piece of something else inserted
here, but its effect on the design is very happy.

PLATE XLIII.   HEAD, FROM ST. MICHAEL'S, SPURRIERGATE, YORK
Fifteenth Century

Some of those in the north aisle are designed on the same plan as the St. William and St. Cuthbert windows, small subject panels arranged in rows. One shows the Six Corporal Acts of Mercy—Feeding the Hungry, Giving Drink to the Thirsty, Receiving Strangers, Clothing the Naked, Visiting the Sick, and Visiting the Prisoners. The little scenes are full of verve and "go," the fifteenth century artist having regained much of the life and vigour which makes the medallions of the Early Period so delightful, with an even greater power of expression. Plate XXXIX. represents the Merciful Man visiting the prisoners in the stocks. I wish Mr. Saint could have found time to have copied the whole of the scene, of which the humour is, I feel sure, not unconscious. Plates XXXVII. and XXXVIII. are from the bottom of this window, and show the donor and his wife with the priest saying mass for them.

Another window illustrates in a number of scenes the Last Fifteen Days of the World, as described in Richard Rolle's *Pricke of Conscience*, and is well calculated to make the evil-doer take thought and mend his ways.

Through the energy of the present rector, a full and careful catalogue and description of all the old glass in the church has been prepared and published. I only wish this were done for the Cathedral and other churches in York, which is richer, perhaps, in the quantity of its old stained glass than any other city in the world.

PLATE XLIV.   HEAD OF AN ARCHBISHOP, CANTERBURY
Fifteenth Century

XV

FIFTEENTH CENTURY GLASS
IN FRANCE

XV

FIFTEENTH CENTURY GLASS
IN FRANCE

THE French school, when it revived in the second
half of the fifteenth century, came, as I have said,
almost at once, and far earlier than the English
school, under the influence of the schools of The influence
painting which had been developed in the Nether- of pictorial
lands (where the Van Eycks were working as early
as 1420), and also, to an extent which has only
been realized comparatively recently, in France
itself.

There was both advantage and disadvantage in
this. The drawing of the French is generally a
little better than our own, and there is more
variety and enterprise in their colour schemes than
in our later Perpendicular work. On the other
hand, it seems to me that almost from the
beginning they were hampered, if ever so little at

243

first, by the desire to apply to glasswork the standards of a different medium.

The difficulty had not arisen before. The illumination or wall painting of the thirteenth and early fourteenth century in England and the north of France could be translated into glass with little change, but, in the fifteenth century, the painters of illuminations and panel pictures had learnt all sorts of things about light and shade and landscape and flesh painting that did not come at all easily to the worker in glass and lead, and were of no help to him in his task of beautifying windows. It was inevitable that he should make some attempt to follow in the cry, and the extent to which he succeeded is amazing; but from henceforth, even where he most succeeds, it is to some extent by a *tour de force*, by a compromise between incompatibilities.

Early fifteenth century work.

For the first part of the century, as I have said, the number of windows produced in France seems to have been few. Such events as the disaster of Agincourt, the conquest of France by Henry V., and its deliverance by Joan of Arc can have left little money or thought for stained-glass windows. The names of the *maîtres verriers* of the cathedrals show that all through the time there

PLATE XLV. HEAD OF PATRIARCH, FROM WINDOW IN SOUTH AISLE OF NAVE,
ST. PATRICE, ROUEN
Fifteenth Century

were men who carried on the tradition, but their output seems to have been small. What windows they have left us do not show the same complete change from the work of the previous century that we find in England; the style did not as in England crystallize into a definite form, but remained as a transitional style between that of the fourteenth and late fifteenth centuries. In its general outlines the design did not at first differ greatly from that of the fourteenth century, but, as in England, the white canopy touched with stain took the place of all others, and there was a general increase in the amount of white in windows. In detail, however, the canopy altered slowly, and it was never as in England reduced to an almost flat pattern by the use of strong line work, but persisted in the attempt to imitate solid stone-work.

It is not till the second half of the century, when the wars were over, and France had settled down to quiet reconstruction under Louis XI., that we find any great revival of the art, and then it is very different to contemporary work in England.

There is a good deal of fifteenth century work still remaining at Rouen, though there seems to be a gap in the list of *maîtres verriers* to the

Cathedral from 1386 to 1426. It was during this gap, however, in the year 1400, that a window, which still remains, was placed in the clerestory of the Cathedral at Evreux. The general plan of this window is that of those later fourteenth century windows in which the whole light was filled with towering canopy work. The canopy differs only slightly in detail from the late fourteenth century type, though there is a more decided attempt at perspective in it, but, like the English work of the time, it is all white, touched with stain, and the general effect of the window is much whiter than that of earlier work. The drawing of the figures, which represent the donor, Bishop Guillaume de Cantier, presented to the Virgin by St. Catherine, does not show any very great change from late fourteenth century work.

Evreux.

St. Ouen at Rouen.

The fifteenth century windows at Rouen follow, for the most part, the general design of the fourteenth century windows in the same churches. Thus the window in the chapel of SS. Peter and Paul in St. Ouen, which Mr. Westlake thinks to be the work of Guillaume Barbe, 1459–85, has much the same arrangement and proportions as the S. Gervais window in the south choir aisle shown in Plate XXV.; that is to say, a small figure panel,

PLATE XLVI. HEAD OF ST. CATHERINE, FROM WINDOW ABOVE ALTAR IN NORTH-WEST
CORNER OF ST. VINCENT'S, ROUEN
Fifteenth Century

PLATE XLVII.   DRAPERY FROM SLEEVE OF VIRGIN, FROM WEST END OF ST VINCENT'S, ROUEN
Fifteenth Century

under a big canopy, is set half-way up each tall light of which the top and bottom is filled with quarries. There is the same coloured background to the canopy, ending at the top in the same arched shape, but in the treatment of the canopy itself one finds a difference not only from fourteenth century work but from English work of the fifteenth century. The French canopy, as I have said, had never, like the English, been reduced to an almost flat pattern of intricate line work, and in these Rouen windows one finds the artist already trying to imitate stone-work modelled in relief with results that are heavy and unsatisfactory. It is not that, in English work, individual shafts are not given a light and dark side, but the canopy is not, as in French work, modelled as a solid whole, and the strong line work seems to keep it right.

It was not, however, till the second half of the century that any new life came into French stained-glass work, and when it came it brought with it a skill in picture-making that was borrowed from contemporary painting. To this period belong, I think, the fragments from Rouen shown in Plates XLV. to XLIX. The heads of St. Catherine and the old man, if compared with those from York, show the strong difference in facial

The revival

type between French and English work at this time. The stain on the hair of St. Catherine is very coarse and inartistic as compared with English work, but then no other nation ever equalled the English in their delicate and refined use of stain.

The two heads of Angels (Plates XLVIII., XLIX.), which are from the north transept of St. Ouen, are, I think, by the same hand as an interesting " Assumption of the Virgin," which now occupies two lights of a window in the north St. Maclou. aisle of St. Maclou in the same city. A significant point about this glass is that the picture, which is enclosed by a wide, flat-arched canopy, delicately modelled, stretches right across both lights, completely ignoring the intervening mullion, one of the first hints that stained glass was forgetting its architectural mission.[1] The composition is much more ambitious and pictorial, and the drawing more advanced than in any of the glass we have hitherto considered. In front is a crowd of kneeling saints in robes of blue, red, and green, above whom the Virgin kneels before the Almighty, while the top of the picture is filled with rows of golden-haired angels with red wings on a blue

---

[1] It is true that the glass is not now in its original position, but I think it must always have filled two lights.

PLATE XLVIII. ANGEL'S HEAD, FROM GREAT ROSE WINDOW IN NORTH TRANSEPT OF ST. OUEN'S, ROUEN

Fifteenth Century

LAWRENCE B.
SAINT 1911

PLATE XLIX.   ANGEL'S HEAD, FROM GREAT ROSE WINDOW IN NORTH TRANSEPT OF ST. OUEN'S, ROUEN

Fifteenth Century

ground, of a similar type to those illustrated. I should put the date of the window at about 1470–80.

Of about the same date are the side windows of the Lady Chapel of the Cathedral at Evreux, of which the building was finished, I believe, in 1475. I am surprised that Mr. Westlake, in his notice of the chapel, only mentions the east window with its Jesse tree, which to me is much less beautiful than the others, and which I should be inclined to attribute, at the earliest, to the very end of the century, if not to the following one. The four side windows tell the story of Christ's Ministry, Passion, and Resurrection, and show His second coming. Their arrangement is somewhat English, each window having two tiers of lights, each of which has a subject enclosed in a white canopy, but the technique is different from the English. By far the best is the first window of the series, which contains eight scenes from the Ministry of Christ, from the Marriage in Cana to the Entry into Jerusalem. The canopy work with its little figures in niches is modelled as Van Eyck might have done it ; the method would not tell well at a distance, but owing to the narrowness of the chapel one cannot get far away from these windows. The figure panels are very rich in colour,

The Lady Chapel at Evreux.

Christ being always dressed in a deep purple, and the other figures in rich greens, blues, and reds. The other windows of the series are not quite so good, being thinner and poorer in effect, and seem to me to have been executed by another hand, possibly from the designs of the author of the first window, who may have died in the interval. There is a good deal of similar work in the church of St. Taurin in the same town.

From the pictorial point of view these windows are much more accomplished than anything that had so far been done in England. In comparing English and French fifteenth century work, however, it must always be remembered that the best English work was done during the first half of the century, and is far better than the French work of that time, whereas the best French work was done in the second half of the century when the English Perpendicular style had for the most part become stereotyped and dull, and seemed to resist the introduction of new ideas. These Evreux windows represent the style which, under the influence of contemporary picture-painting, was growing up on the Continent, but which did not obtain a foothold in England till the advent, almost at the end of the century, of the school which produced the Fairford windows.

XVI

MALVERN AND FAIRFORD

XVI

MALVERN AND FAIRFORD

So great was the quantity of stained glass produced in England in the fifteenth century, and so much still remains, that it is impossible, in this book, even to mention all the more important examples. We have seen the growth and perfection of the Perpendicular style at York. At Great Malvern Priory you may study its gradual decadence.

The best of the windows there are undoubtedly the earliest, namely, those in St. Anne's Chapel which include the famous "Creation," of which the date is perhaps 1440–50. It cannot, I think, compare with John Thornton's "Creation" in the east window of York Minster,—the colour scheme is so much more conventional and less expressive, —but it is nevertheless very beautiful. The resemblance of some of the scenes to those in Thornton's window is perhaps no more than one

Great Malvern: the "Creation."

253

would expect to find in two representations of the same subject in the same period, but at the same time the Malvern "Creation" is very much akin to York work, though rather to the later phase represented by the St. Cuthbert and the All Saints' windows, than to the work of Thornton. I may be wrong, but I sometimes suspect that the inhabitants of the Severn and Avon valleys had more intercourse with the North of England—to which access would be easy by the Avon and Trent, navigable most of the way—than with the Thames Valley and South of England, from which they were cut off by the wild and inhospitable Cotswolds.

In comparing the later windows in Malvern Priory with the "Creation" and its neighbours in St. Anne's Chapel, one can trace a decided and increasing decadence. The forms are the same but stereotyped and dull, the artists seem timid in their use of colour, and all the life seems to go out The north of the style. The great north transept window, transept given in 1501–2 by Henry VII. (it once contained window. his portrait and still has that of his son Prince Arthur and the architect, Sir Reginald Bray), is, compared with the earlier work, a very poor affair. The yellow stain in particular is very coarse and

overdone, yet such was the hold which this style
had got on our countrymen that in spite of the
late date of the window there is not a hint in it of
the new ideas which were then coming in, although
it is probable that before it was finished, the
famous windows of Fairford, not forty miles away
across the Cotswolds, had at least been begun.

The old church of Fairford with its square *Fairford.*
central tower, standing on a green slope above a
rushing trout stream, which, a few miles below,
unites with the baby Thames and makes it a
navigable river, occupies a unique position, not
merely as the only village church in England—
one may, perhaps, say in the world—which still
retains the whole of its original set of stained-glass
windows almost intact, but from the quality of
the windows themselves.   Some, it is true, have
suffered damage, but there is not a subject unrecog-
nizable, nor a window missing.

The church was begun by John Tame, merchant
of London, and finished by his son, Sir Edward;
but since John Tame's will, dated 1496, while
bequeathing various sums for ornaments to the
church, makes no mention of the glass, it is argued
that the glass had been already ordered.   The
Fairford windows are usually classed as Per-

pendicular on the strength of their association with
Perpendicular architecture and the presence of
Perpendicular detail in the canopies and elsewhere,
but it is a wholly different style to the Perpendicular of York, of Malvern, of Warwick; the
style which, with little change, had held the field
in England since the beginning of the century.
Fairford, in fact, marks a revolution in English
stained glass.   It is an early, if not the first work
of a new school which, throwing away the old
native tradition, based its style on that which had
grown up on the Continent and, still more, upon
Flemish painting.   The Fairford windows represent a phase of their art which did not last very
long, for their style soon began to assimilate itself
to that of the Renaissance.   In the windows of
King's College Chapel at Cambridge you may see
the change happening, and in the latest windows
there you may also, alas! see the rapid setting in
of decadence.   It was, indeed, a style which
contained in itself the seeds of decay, which
germinated all too rapidly ; but these, its first-fruits,
at Fairford are magnificent, and disarm criticism.

They mark, as I say, a complete departure from
the older standards of English fifteenth century
glass.   It is the same story, once more repeated, of

The new
style.

old conventions of drawing becoming out of date, and failing to satisfy a newer generation. Of the more advanced schools of painting, the Flemish was the one that Englishmen were most in touch with, and it was thence that the new school of English glass-workers took their inspiration, with the result that a Flemish feeling is traceable in all their work. One immediate result of the more pictorial standard now expected of the artist was that he came to depend in quite a different way on the painting of his glass as distinct from the glazing. At Fairford, elaborate landscape backgrounds are put in with the brown enamel alone, helped by yellow stain, sometimes on white, sometimes on grey-blue glass, to which latter the stain gives a green for grass and trees. Not as yet, however, does the painting take precedence of the glazing, the balance being for a time held equal between the two. Indeed the craft of glazing, as well as that of painting, was now at its height; the artist had all the resources of both at his command and used them to the full, but as yet the limits of the medium were not overstepped.

Another result of the pictorial standard now arrived at, was that the artist began to feel cramped by the narrow lights he had to fill, and to let his

17

subjects spread through more than one of them, ignoring the intervening mullion.   At Fairford many of the subjects occupy two lights, and the " Crucifixion " at the east end and the " Doom " at the west spread right across the whole width of the window.   As yet this is not so done that one loses the sense of the design decorating the stone-work ; but both these developments are indications of a tendency which was to increase as time went on, and eventually to ruin the art.

The new point of view naturally affected the canopy, which is shaded like solid stone-work, giving it a heavy and clumsy effect.   In many of the subject windows, however, the canopy is omitted altogether, the sky of the picture, which is some-times white, with clouds and circling swifts painted on it, continuing right up to the stone-work.

The problem of the author- ship of the windows.

I agree with Mr. Westlake in finding the work of more than one hand in the windows.   Two there are certainly, and possibly four.   The east window is certainly by a different, and, I think, an older hand than the west, and the windows of the north aisle, though they may be by the same hand as the west windows, are certainly by a different one to the Apostles opposite them, which are the poorest windows in the church.   I think the differences are

PLATE L. THE PROPHETS JOEL, ZEPHANIAH, AMOS, AND HOSEA,
FROM THE NORTH AISLE OF THE NAVE, FAIRFORD
Late Fifteenth Century

greater than could be accounted for by any development that might take place in the same man's style during the execution of the windows. The west windows are the work of a different temperament to the east windows. The forms are fuller, stronger, and more rounded, and show a much stronger sense for the decorative placing of a line.

There is no record to tell us who these men were, and there has been much discussion as to whether they were Englishmen or Flemings. Indeed the wildest theories have been advanced as to the origin of the windows. They have been attributed to Dürer, without the slightest internal or external evidence except the presence of an A which does not resemble his signature. Another story which, though not heard of, I believe, till the eighteenth century, has obtained wide credence, is that they were captured at sea, bound for Rome, by Edward Tame, and the church built to contain them; but the most casual examination of the windows ought to convince any one that they were made for the church and not the church for them.[1]

As to the question of the English or Flemish

---

[1] This is fully gone into by Canon Carbonel in an article in *Memorials of Old Gloucestershire*. Another theory he examines and rejects is that they were the work of the Dutch painter Aeps.

authorship of the windows, it is true that Flemish details crop up here and there both in architecture and the costumes ; but this is not surprising, for the style, new then to England, was largely based on Flemish art, and on the other hand the English characteristics are in excess of the Flemish.

In Henry VII.'s Chapel at Westminster, high up in the central clerestory window of the apse, is a single figure under a canopy which bears a most striking resemblance to the series of the Prophets at Fairford (Plate L.).   In the figure, in the scroll he holds, in the canopy, in the treatment of the drapery, and even in the queer drawing of the hands, the resemblance is so close that I for one cannot doubt their common authorship.   Now it is on record that the windows of Henry VII.'s Chapel

Barnard Flower.

were glazed by "one Barnard Flower," the king's glazier, who also is the glazier named in the first contract for the windows in King's College Chapel at Cambridge, but who died in 1525–26 before they were finished.   A comparison of those windows at Cambridge which are believed to be his work, especially that over the north door, with the Fairford windows, reveals many points of resemblance, and, allowing for the twenty years which probably separate the execution of the two

works, I think we should not be far wrong in
assigning to Flower the whole of the north aisle at
Fairford, and perhaps the Latin Fathers in the
south aisle. Whether the west windows are his
work too I do not feel sure, and to the names of
the other artists who took part in the work we have
no clue.

Yet though one may thus trace various hands The general
in the work, the windows form a connected whole, scheme.
the planning of which must have been the work of
one mind. The arrangement is the traditional one
whereby the whole church forms an exposition of
the foundations of the Christian faith. The
windows of the nave contain single figures, the
Prophets on the north side (Plate L.) facing the
Apostles on the south. Each Apostle holds a verse
of the creed, and the Prophet opposite him a
corresponding verse from his writings. The four
Evangelists face the four Latin Fathers. Farther
east, within the now vanished screen, the windows
unfold the Gospel story, those on the north leading
up to the Passion in the east window, those on the
south showing the Descent into Hell, the Resurrection, and the events that followed. Then, as the
spectator turns to the west, there faces him, in the The
great west window, the tremendous " Doom " or " Doom."

Last Judgment.   Do not look at the upper half where Christ sits enthroned as Judge, surrounded by saints and angels ; it has suffered the fate of the Winchester College glass.   Blown in by a storm in 1703, it was "restored" in the middle of the nineteenth century, which means that the old glass was removed and a bad copy substituted.   Where the blue ring of Heaven passes through the tracery lights the original glass remains, and the difference between it and the new is an object lesson in good and bad stained-glass work.

But below the transom the window is still unspoilt.   In the midst stands Michael with sword and scales, and below him the dead are rising naked from their graves.   Michael himself, it must be confessed, is a somewhat lackadaisical figure ; it was not possible for an artist of that time and school to give a figure the arresting quality of the Methuselah in Plate III. ; neither does one's eye linger long over the Saved, who troop up the golden stairs on Michael's right, but is irresistibly attracted to the other side of the picture, where in a great glow of ruby glass are seen the Flames of Hell, to which devils—grey and blue at the outer edge of the fire, but darker and more purple as they are farther in—are carrying the wretched souls of the Lost. Just outside the flames an angel and a devil are fighting in mid-air for the possession of a soul, and a comparison of these figures with the similar ones in the Descent into Limbo or " Harrying of Hell," which is by the same hand as the east window, shows at once the difference between the work of the two men.

On either side the west windows of the aisles contain, as types of the Last Judgment, on the north, the Judgment of Solomon, which protected the innocent; on the south, that of David on the Amalekite, which condemned the guilty. It seems to me not unlikely that the position of these windows was originally reversed, Solomon's judgment being on the side of the Saved in the " Doom" and David's on that of the Lost. They have both suffered greatly in the storm of 1703 and contain many blank spaces, but from what remains they seem to me, together with the " Doom," the most accomplished work in the church. *The west windows of the aisles.*

Very splendid, too, are the Persecutors of the Church, who, clad in all the bravery of wickedness, fill the north side of the clerestory, fronting the somewhat insipid row of Martyrs on the other side. Here is Herod transfixing an Innocent; Nero, *The clerestory.*

if it is he, with the head of St. Paul; the King of the Huns, and Diocletian, perhaps, with bows and arrows; and, in a dark blue robe, Judas, with the halter round his neck and the bag in his hand, between Annas and Caiaphas. In the tracery lights above the Martyrs are rather commonplace white and gold angels, but over the Persecutors are fascinating little figures of devils, grey, blue, and green, on a background of ruby flames. I am afraid there is no question which series the artist enjoyed doing most!

Fairford marks the end of mediæval stained glass in England. Conservative artists might still, as at Malvern and at St. Neots in Cornwall, try to carry on the older tradition, but their works are isolated survivals. The Fairford windows themselves represent, as I have said, a very short-lived phase in English glass, of which they are the most complete example, others being the fragments in Henry VII.'s Chapel at Westminster and the remains of Bishop Fox's glazing in Winchester Cathedral, now collected into the east clerestory window there. Flower's own work at King's College, Cambridge, twenty years later than Fairford, shows signs of change, and that of his successors in the same building, as at Basingstoke, at Balliol College and elsewhere must be classed as wholly of the Renaissance.   With Fairford, then, these notes on Stained Glass of the Middle Ages may fitly end.

INDEX

THE END

Printed in Great Britain by R. & R. CLARK, LIMITED, *Edinburgh.*